TWO
PHA

FIVE
BILLION
SLAVES

•••

TWO HUNDRED PHARAOHS
PHARAOHS
FIVE
BILLION
SLAVES

ADRIAN
PEACOCK

●●●ellipsis

All rights reserved. No part of this publication may be reproduced in any form without the prior written permission of the copyright holders / First published 1999 by Repetitive Fame Injury Press / This edition published 2002 by ●●●ellipsis / Copyright © 2002 Adrian Peacock / Introduction copyright © 2002 Gavin Turk / British Library Cataloguing in Publication / A CIP record for this book is available from the British Library / ISBN 1 84166 071 x / Design by Claudia Schenk / Printed in Finland / ●●●ellipsis is a registered trade mark of Ellipsis London Limited / 2 Rufus Street, London N1 6PE / www.ellipsis.com / For a copy of the Ellipsis catalogue or information on special quantity orders of Ellipsis books please contact sales on 020 7739 3157 or sales@ellipsis.co.uk

CONTENTS

INTRODUCTION by Gavin Turk / 1 1

THEM / 1 3
Post-Utopia / The bourgeoisie: the world's bosses / The
global middle class / The dialectic / Bourgeois
revolution: France 1789 / Contradictions of the feudal
system / Abolition of the feudal class system /
The revolutionary nation / Class consciousness /
The precocity of revolutionary consciousness: England
1381 and Paris 1871

THE STRUGGLE / 3 7
Towards abolition of the fluid class system / The
reproduction of class society / The making of a global
working class / Proletarian revolution: France 1968 /
The need for a new revolutionary movement / The
poverty of alienation in a world of abundance /
Monopoly and surplus / Monopoly capitalist society /

TWO HUNDRED PHARAOHS

The welfare state internationalised / War /
Militarism and labour discipline / Our revolutionary
project revives

US / 6 1
Solidarity / The proletariat: a global industrial working
class / As consumers / The proletarian pseudo-middle
class / The peasantry

THE STALEMATE / 7 1
Revolutionary bourgeoisie in the 20th century / Marxist
bourgeoisies / Proletarianised bourgeois revolution:
Russia 1917 / Bolshevism / Stalinism / All power stolen
from the workers' councils / A trade route to a new
working class / Bourgeois parliamentary democracy /
Nazi Revolution: Germany 1933

THE HAMSTER WHEEL / 9 0
The early factory system / Social progress as a
by-product of the factory system / Strikes / Trades
unions / Syndicalism / Socialism

FASTER!! / 1 0 9
The next phase of the bourgeois revolution / Early
capitalism: the formal subsumption of labour under
capital / Subsumption theory / Industrial capitalism:
the real subsumption of labour under capital /
Cybernetic capitalism: the real subsumption of leisure
under capital

SHOPPING / 1 1 6
The subsumption of the high street / Towards leisure

discipline / Consumerism: mass realisation /
Mega-malls / The impact of mega-malls / The
mega-mall as the beginnings of real subsumption of
leisure under capital / Leisure planning / 'Lifestyle'
and cybernetic shopping / Globalisation of the factory
system / Cybernetic capitalism: the subsumption of
Fordism

CONTESTING UNCLE GEORGE'S WILL   **/ 1 3 7**
Hegel: the Moses of the pyramid scheme / The theory
of bourgeois revolution / The theory of democratic
history / Hegel and revolution / Hegelian theory of
revolution / Hegelian contradictions for the
bourgeoisie / The recurrent end of history / Refutation
of Hegel during confrontational periods / The global
spirit of history (the 'world soul') / Hegel
deconstructed / Nationalism / Capitalist globalisation
after 1989 / World bourgeois revolution

FAIRYTALES   **/ 1 5 8**
World proletarian revolution / The proletariat
announces its programme: the abolition of capitalism /
Classless or 'communist' society / Work in classless
society / Communist crises / The centralisation of
capital / Towards a global Paris Commune / Growing
negation: Albanian revolution 1997 / The fresh
possibility of revolution in the advanced economies /
American revolution: 21st century

LET'S BUILD A ROCKET   **/ 1 7 7**
Towards a revolutionary organisation / The dictatorship
of the proletariat / Workers' councils / Catalysts /

TWO HUNDRED PHARAOHS

Spontaneity / Practical activity / The revolutionary
organisation / Total democracy / Theory of the workers'
movement

CARPETBAGGERS   / 1 9 1
The new left / False contestation / The cult of
Kronstadt / Bourgeois revolutionary middle
management / Anarchism / The Spanish revolution 1936
/ Anarchist moralism / Anarchist ministers /
Anarcho-environmentalism / Against the appearance of
councilist ideology / Situationism (the last form of
ideology) / Islamic revolution: Iran 1978

CLOWNS   / 2 1 5
False consciousness / Senior academics / Radical
academics / Radical academic monologue /
Structuralism / Post-structuralism / Postmodernism /
Fame

SUPERSTARS   / 2 3 1
Pseudo-revolutionary literature / Our great adventure /
Homo sparticus /

**I want to be
an anarchist
but my parents
aren't rich
enough**

IF ART COULD BE SEEN AS A
MIRROR STANDING ONE STEP
AWAY FROM AND REFLECTING
SOCIETY, SIMILARLY THE
REVOLUTION, IN CHALLENGING
CULTURAL HEGEMONY, EXPOSES
AND ENABLES US TO CATCH A
GLIMPSE OF OUR SOCIETY. 'HASTA
LA VICTORIA SIEMPRE.'

GAVIN TURK

Planet-owners Fahd and Waleed Bin Tallal
are too drunk to notice when their
chauffeurs build them a wicker-man
out of passenger jets in New York

THEM

Post-Utopia

> Reality is superseding Utopia. There is no longer any point in projecting an imaginary bridge between the richness of present technological capacities and the poverty of their use by the capitalist ruling class. We want to put society's material equipment at the disposal of everyone's creativity as the masses themselves always strive to do in the moment of revolution.[1]

Today the productive capacity of the human race is such that it is possible for us to feed the world's entire population dozens of times over; to clothe everyone in the latest fashions; to cure or prevent most of the world's debilitating diseases; to house everyone in luxurious accommodation and pleasant cities; to communicate freely with each other; and, more than all this, to turn humanity's long-cherished dreams into social reality. In short, the conditions already exist for us to build a world better than Utopia.

1 *Situationist International* 9, 1964.

And so mighty are the productive powers we possess that all these facilities can be provided virtually free of charge. Indeed, so effortless is modern society's ability to mass-produce that there is a constant struggle to destroy, dilute and prevent from being created in the first place such an abundance of food and manufactured goods that their prices sink to next to nothing and they become impossible to sell.

Technology is now so advanced that the working week could occupy minutes rather than hours, supplying every material need and leaving us to pose as physical Hercules or intellectual Einsteins. It can give us all-seeing eyes with which to examine distant planets, or the intricacies of life, or the sub-atomic particles of reality itself.

Yet amazingly, despite these powers, we live in a world not dominated by genius and heroism, but by poverty, hunger, fear, boredom and ignorance. No gadget will ever be invented to help us to resolve this contradiction. The solution lies within ourselves. The incredible potential of our world can only be united with our imagination as a species if we manage to evolve our social organisation beyond the prehistoric stage of capitalism.

This is no idle wish or academic project: industrial capitalism is the system which has brought about the immense possibilities outlined above. It is the most revolutionary and dynamic form yet taken by human society but as it unites us it challenges us to overthrow it because it is owned by a tiny elite who are its ultimate beneficiaries.

Our society cannot continue without that elite forcing us to work harder and harder for them with less and less say over what we create or what we enjoy. Industrial capitalism functions by recreating a more intensely unequal world for us to survive in than the one it starts with. This is because capitalism is a gigantic worldwide pyramid scheme that functions on the basis of a social hierarchy extended across the entire planet. The result is a polarised world in which all the benefits of industrial production, such as they are, have accrued internationally to the populations of just a handful of leading economies and only to the top ten per cent among them at best.

> It is estimated that the additional cost of achieving and maintaining universal access to basic education, health care, maternity care, adequate food, safe water and sanitation for the whole human race is roughly $40 billion a year. This is less than four per cent of the combined wealth of the 225 richest people.[2]

This concentration represents only a fraction of the world's real wealth, however. Towering above it are the lost innovations and potential never realised by the vast bulk of the human race because virtually all of us are denied a say in the running of society or the purposes of production. And so we all, 'rich' and poor alike, live in a world of dreadful poverty dominated by waste and haunted by lost opportunities.

The bourgeoisie: the world's bosses

The rich, the bourgeoisie, are the owners and controllers of the world's multinational monopolies. They are the majority share- and bond-holders and therefore the ultimate recipients of nearly all of the world's surplus value – and the power that this bestows.

They are the world's ruling class, a class comprising just a few hundred billionaires. Practically all of them are industrialists or retailers of one type or another. A few epitomise the system as a

---

2 'The Rich and Poor Grow Further Apart', United Nations Report quoted in *The Guardian*, 9 September 1998.

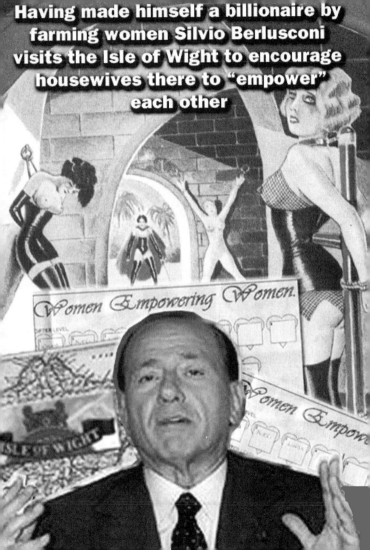

Having made himself a billionaire by farming women Silvio Berlusconi visits the Isle of Wight to encourage housewives there to "empower" each other

whole by simply promoting enormous pyramid schemes (for example The American Way International), but whatever the initial source of their profits all of them must continually reinvest across the entire capitalist system in order to remain in the elite.

Because of its pyramid structure this process of reinvestment demands that the rich risk substantial amounts of their wealth on new ventures– they have to anticipate the technological or political changes that might otherwise sweep their rivals into power. It is this that makes them the international owners of the means of production.

Their wealth during the 1990s created global levels of hierarchy and inequality more extreme than those which, when merely national, triggered the French Revolution of the 1790s:

> ... according to the United Nations, the 225 richest people in the world have a combined wealth of more than $1 trillion – equal to the annual income of the poorest 47 per cent of the earth's population, some 2.5 billion people – the three richest men on the planet have assets that exceed the combined GDP of the 48 least developed countries.[3]

So vast have the profits from industrialisation become that the scale of bourgeois wealth is almost beyond comprehension. Most of the apparently super-wealthy in each nation (men who can afford to spend more than £13,000 on a single meal, for example),[4] though they seem to be phenomenally rich, are merely 'middle class', the underling servants of the real bourgeoisie.

The global polarisation between rich and poor is repeated within

3 ibid.
4 'Dinner for Three? Not the wine you want, but a bargain at £13,091' (description of businessmen's lunch at Le Gavroche to celebrate a business deal), *Evening Standard*, 17 November 1997.

most nations but is most highly concentrated in the leading economy of America, where less than one per cent of the population controls more than 40 per cent of the national wealth with a handful of billionaires amongst that one per cent also controlling a similar share of the world's wealth.

In the USA it is now estimated that the average major company director earns 170 times more money than the average worker. This has prompted one commentator to write:

> there is no doubt that the biggest winners, by far, during the past two decades have been the people who control the means of production: company directors and shareholders.[5]

No better illustration of the modern scale of genuine bourgeois wealth and power can be found than to quote from a financial-newspaper article on the 'mega-rich' of America, prompted by an American billionaire's gift to the United Nations:

> With one swipe of a pen Microsoft founder Bill Gates could wipe out the US government deficit ... Many American individuals now have access to more money than state governments. Media mogul Ted Turner can give away $1 billion to the United Nations and still be wealthy enough to remain in the top 400 richest Americans ... the debate should not be what is wrong with America that a rich man feels it necessary to step into the government's role by funding the UN but why he is so wealthy that he can. These wealthy people owe the world, especially the US and its government. They are wealthy beyond belief because economic growth and investment patterns have changed in favour of Wall Street ... What is wrong is that normal folk and governments should bow down before the generosity of

5 John Cassidy, 'The Next Big Thinker', *The New Yorker/Independent on Sunday*, 7 December 1997.

those who have benefited most from current economic expansion. Government policies and economic trends that have driven up stocks and enriched the wealthy have not improved the lives of those at the bottom of the economic chain … the billionaires should thank the government and everyone else on whose backs their economic miracles were made.[6]

It is impossible to make a better case for revolution than this, except to say that the billionaires own the world rather than owe it and that they would be baffled as to why they should thank governments which have merely been carrying out their orders.

We must recognise in the power of the billionaires our own immense power, in alienated form, which becomes ours as soon as we embark on a full-scale proletarian revolution.

The global middle class

At the global level the term 'middle class' is a misnomer. So steep is the hierarchical pinnacle at the apex of the world's class system that the independent share-, bond- and landowners who appear just beneath the summit of the world's true billionaire owners are so unequal in their access to power and wealth that they do not make up any recognisable class;[7] except that, as the entourage of the bourgeoisie, they will readily act as its adoring fan-club (sometimes visibly in the form of shareholder claques applauding the boards of the multinationals at annual general meetings).

6 Lauren Chambliss, 'Why the mega-rich should thank picketing workers', *Business Day, Evening Standard*, 1 October 1997.

7 While there are approximately nine million 'dollar-millionaires' on earth (0.15 per cent of the human race), there are just 55,000 people worth $30 million or more in liquid assets, according to Merrill Lynch, Cap Gemini (*MLCG World Wealth Report 2000*).

Richard Grasso, head of the New York Stock Exchange, meets the leader of the Columbian Marxists to fix the price of cocaine for the coming year. (26.6.99)

Collectively, the middle classes are those who appear as the main minority shareholders on the share registers of the world. In normal times they can be expected to assist in crushing us, the workers. However, because the bourgeoisie is a dynamic class, some of them will eagerly take (or fund) revolutionary action if they see an opportunity to step into the shoes of the super-rich majority shareholders above them.

The middle class contains many transitory figures who are benefiting from the pockets of the world economy yet to be made fully capitalist, and so they retain feudal or military power not derived completely from wealth. These are the detritus of aristocratic families, royal remnants and the leaders of religions. Propping up these anachronisms wherever it still suits the imperialist needs of Western states are the world's government agents immune from prosecution, senior diplomats (including the upper echelons of the security services) and their mafiosi responsible for most of the world's drug trade.

They are mixed in with the coat-tailing flunkies and butlers of the rich: service industrialists, university professors, generals, high-ranking civil servants, pop, sports and media stars, former wives and families, some still-existing slave owners and other parasites. Their main purpose is to advertise the 'benefits' of an unequal society by making the shoddy world of monopoly look glamorous, accessible and democratic while reinforcing the idea that authority, beauty, intelligence and expertise are all attributes of wealth. Most of the world's university students are drawn from this class which is why references to 'student revolutions' in the mass media are laughable.

As much as it can be said to constitute a class at all, the middle class currently makes up less than 10 per cent of the world's population and is rarely as much as 15 per cent in any given country.

On some estimates the 'middle class' in the world's most

polarised society, America, which of course stands at the top of the economic pyramid and so represents the future polarisation of all other countries, now amounts to little more than 3 per cent of the population (around two million families). In Britain only 8 per cent of the workforce earned more than £26,100 per annum (the 40 per cent tax threshold) in 1998, and only 7 per cent have been educated privately. This reflects the astronomical rates of loss inherent to pyramid-schemes.

Yet the interests of the 'middle classes' are always represented in bourgeois society as being those of the political 'middle ground' which is supposed to constitute the majority of the population.

The rich therefore regard democracy as the need to respect the interests of those catching the sizeable crumbs from their banqueting table, the minority shareholders of their companies. Honouring the interests of the real majority, the workers who produce their companies' wealth, would, of course, destroy them as a class.

In the long term, however, capitalism is dedicated to eradicating the middle classes as surely as it wishes to see an end to the peasantry. The size of today's middle classes is dramatically down on the 20 per cent of the population that was the usual national average half a century ago. Each major economic crisis reduces their numbers still further while demonstrating the lie behind the regular and juvenile announcements of bourgeois society that it has 'made everyone middle class' through the free distribution of shares, mortgages, lottery winnings, etc., to the working population. The scope of these catchpenny schemes is ludicrously limited when compared to the awesome scale of the bourgeoisie's real global property holdings. These occasional confetti-sized gifts from governments convey no social power whatsoever to the smattering of workers who can afford to hold on to them.

The dialectic

Two hundred years ago one of the earliest working-class theorists of modern industrial society described how the dialectic of capitalism would both polarise our world and liberate us:

> a sort of Socratic spirit will necessarily grow up, wherever large bodies of workers assemble … Monopoly, and the hideous accumulation of capital in a few hands … carry in their enormity, the seeds of cure. Whatever presses us together, though it may generate some vices, is favourable to the diffusion of knowledge, and ultimately promotive of human liberty. Hence every large workshop and manufactory is a sort of political society, which no act of parliament can silence, and no magistrate disperse.[8]

This belief, that the bourgeoisie's industrial capitalism makes itself ever more vulnerable as it strives to assemble an ever larger and more integrated working class to exploit by inadvertently promoting unity and consciousness among us, is the central theory of the revolutionary workers' movement. It inspires our movement to analyse the 'laws of motion' of capitalist expansion the better to understand how to turn 'expanded and aggrandised workshops' into a 'society promotive of human liberty'.

Because, despite the social inequality it currently generates, industrial capitalism is predicated upon assumptions of revolutionary democracy and co-operation which we can turn into the basis of society itself. In this way our revolutionary project as workers, the lowest class under capitalism, seeks to complete what was

8 John Thelwall, *The Rights of Nature*, 1797 (quoted by E P Thompson, The *Making of the English Working Class*, 1968). Thelwall was the chief theorist of the London Corresponding Society (1792–99), a society which 'has the distinction of being, in all probability, the first political organisation of the working class.' (Poulsen, *English Rebels*, 1984).

begun by our predecessors, the lowest class under feudalism whose victory placed some of them in control of our world.

Although the bourgeoisie tower above us today as economic dictators their system of domination differs from every previous form of oppression. Through its actions it still holds out the prospect of total freedom for the human race. Because the bourgeoisie emerged from the first triumphant insurrection by a revolutionary underclass in history, 'it is the only revolutionary class that has ever been victorious.'[9]

The bourgeoisie seized hold of one of the most advanced nations of the feudal world in 1789 in the name of unity, freedom and equality and launched the anti-feudalist rebellion now named after its members, the 'bourgeois revolution'. It is this revolution which signposts the path to our freedom too because:

> the bourgeois revolution is a *fait accompli*. Our proletarian revolution is a project, formulated on the basis of the earlier revolution but differing qualitatively from it. To neglect the originality of the bourgeoisie's historical role serves only to conceal the concrete originality of our project, which can get no-where unless it advances under its own banner and comes to grips with the 'prodigiousness of its own aims'. The bourgeoisie came to power because it was the class of the developing economy. We will never come to embody power unless we become the *class of consciousness*.[10]

Today's revolutionary project therefore aims at nothing less than to launch a global anti-capitalist rebellion by seizing control of the most advanced sectors of the capitalist world in the name of the final underclass in history. Because this 'world proletarian revolu-

9 Guy Debord, *The Society of the Spectacle*, 1967.
10 ibid.

tion' can seek nothing but the total abolition of class society as its
goal we will thus realise the highest dreams of human happiness
and freedom, made possible by the dazzling achievement of the
bourgeois revolution.

That revolution inaugurated the process of freeing the human
race from our prehistoric condition of enforced ignorance, false
scarcity and rigid hierarchy, but having done so is now distorting
that process and holding it in check. The story of the bourgeoisie's
victory is a map towards our future liberation as a species.

Bourgeois revolution: France 1789

On a sultry night in Paris two centuries ago representatives of the
world's first successful revolutionary class, after sitting in session
into the small hours, emerged to announce that, from the stately
promontory of their new Assembly, they had 'destroyed the feudal
regime entirely'.

With this summit the 'revolutionary bourgeoisie', the most
advanced members of what was then officially still the peasant
underclass, launched the first social revolution of the masses. They
brought the rest of the class from which they were emerging (the
working people) into the struggle for universal citizenship.

From this titanic upheaval the bourgeoisie were to surface,
bloodied, triumphant, but separated from the masses as a new ruling class in a new type of society, a society no longer based on the
stagnant preservation of ancient privileges (despised by all working
people) but on the dynamic accumulation of projected future
wealth. This society is the society of the revolutionary free citizen
dedicated to accumulating individual private wealth now known as
'capitalist society'.

This first successful revolution of the masses was defined by its
aims: to abolish an undemocratic system of privilege and arrogant

power, to replace a class system based on birth with a society based on merit, and to replace a kingdom of subservient subjects with a nation of free citizens. Because of these ideals the revolution has come to be termed the 'bourgeois revolution' and it established the abolition of class society as the achievable goal of all future social revolutions. However, as a new class, broken free from the workers, the bourgeoisie only abolished the class society of feudalism in relation to the new system of values their emergence represented – economics.

Contradictions of the feudal system

By 1788 the government of France, then one of the world's most advanced societies, was encountering a fiscal crisis from which there seemed to be no escape. The taxation needed to rescue the state from bankruptcy under the growing threat of invasion had become uncollectable since, under the still prevailing feudal regime, the social imperatives were not economic but rigidly hierarchical.

Balancing budgets was not the intended purpose of what existed of central government ('the Court').[11] After all, this would have implied the fundamentally post-feudal and democratic concept that the citizens of a nation were somehow collectively responsible for their future economic well-being.

Feudalism maintained that subjects had to honour and obey their God-given absolute monarch to whom they belonged and who alone could ensure salvation on their behalf. The government was therefore expected to preserve the status quo (God's order) and administer a system of servile deference bestowing privileges which maintained the balance of inequality. These privileges came

---

11 The budget of March 1788 presented to the king was the first, and last, in the
entire feudal period.

increasingly to be represented by the bestowing of a single, routine honour, the right to be exempt from taxes.

A class of merchant peasants which had arisen during the eighteenth century were demanding a corresponding say in the running of the country to that enjoyed by the feudal nobility. As this was impossible within a feudal system, where access to power was determined by birth alone (and these rich merchants were the descendants of the poor), the royal court instead bought them off by extending to them the most basic feudal privilege, that of being tax exempt.

As a result, the contradiction facing the French government could not have been more stark: in order to keep the social system afloat it was being required to waive ever more budgetary restraint and grant broader and broader swathes of tax exemption as a sop to those demanding political influence to match the scale of their wealth. But to keep the country economically and militarily viable it was precisely these newly wealthy citizens whom the state urgently needed to tax in order to stave off collapse. In short feudal France was facing a post-feudal crisis. It was a society structurally unable to comprehend a crisis in the economy as it could only recognise as a crisis a dynastic dispute over succession to the throne.

After a series of skilful accounting tricks had finally been exhausted, the French finance minister Jacques Necker informed the king that the only way forward was to call his subjects together and discuss a way out of the impasse. The king duly announced that a general council would be called for the first time since 1614, a 'grand parlement' or delegation from all areas of the country with the delegates rigidly divided into social orders linked to the system of land-ownership and absolute religion. As these orders were the feudal equivalent of social classes the central tenet of revolutionary theory, that the internal contradictions of class society will force it to establish its own 'negation', was thus first elaborated neither by Hegel nor Marx but by a conservative official of the feudal French court.

Abolition of the feudal class system

The special parliament called was the 'Estates General'. It was an ancient and rarely used mechanism which, dating as it did from the middle ages, was designed only to deal with the economy in medieval terms (to assist the king in deciding who he would honour by exempting them from taxes). It reflected the medieval class system as it was divided into fixed orders who were represented in accordance with their inherited land ownership (or lack of it) or their position in the Church.

This decaying and rudimentary class system was officially known as the 'system of the estates'. These estates were hierarchical and based on the hereditary principle of genealogy. The nobility were at the top (with the king above them all), the clergy made up the second estate, while merchants, peasants, workers and the poor (people of 'lowly birth') were lumped together in a vast underclass, the so-called 'third estate'. Although the third estate represented 96 per cent of the population it was allowed no more than 33 per cent of the votes in any feudal assembly. It could therefore always be out voted by the other two estates.

But this medieval class system had become decrepit. Some profligate nobles were by now impoverished (although they still held land) and, though still officially members of the noble order, were actually among the poor. Meanwhile, many successful peasants and artisans had become so wealthy they were now supporting the French state with loan capital but were still being classed as members of the third estate.

To complicate matters further the middle estate in the social order, the Clergy, contained both very rich members of the upper

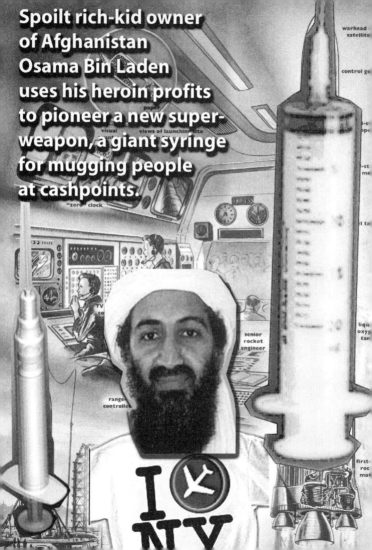

Spoilt rich-kid owner of Afghanistan Osama Bin Laden uses his heroin profits to pioneer a new super-weapon, a giant syringe for mugging people at cashpoints.

clergy and very poor and even revolutionary parish priests. When the Estates General was assembled the wealthy peasants – locked by birth into the social dustbin of the third estate – proclaimed that genealogy was no longer a valid basis for an ossified class system. Instead, they announced that their underclass, the third estate, was now the only universal class. The other estates were abolished; their members had to accept being absorbed into the third estate or face being outlawed.

The revolutionaries proclaimed that all French people regardless of birth now enjoyed the status of free-born citizen ('bourgeois'), a status which had previously existed only as an honour bestowed by the king on some merchant peasants in chartered feudal towns.

In other words, the most conscious members of the third estate declared that the bourgeois citizenship they had been granted under feudalism was henceforth a universal civil right and no longer a feudal privilege. They announced in effect that they were not owned by a king but owned by themselves. In doing this the wealthy peasants of the French revolution established the principle goal of social revolution, the abolition of class society.

The revolutionary nation

In place of a feudal royal family who were the owners of the people, the victorious bourgeoisie erected the revolutionary concept of the 'nation' that was owned by the people and established nationalism as the vehicle for a new, popular form of government.

National loyalty became the ideology of the bourgeois revolution. The concept of the nation meant the hard-won freedoms of the chartered medieval towns would expand to become universal, encompassing an entire country (and eventually an entire planet), throughout which everyone would enjoy the right of free trade.

The bourgeoisie issued their nationalist manifesto at the begin-

ning of their revolution. The pamphlet *What is the Third Estate?*
(1789) answered its rhetorical question thus:

> What is the Third Estate? – Everything.
> What has it been till now in the political order? Nothing.
> What does it desire to be? Something.
> … Who would deny that the Third Estate has within itself all that is
> necessary to constitute a nation? Take away the privileged orders, and the
> nation is not smaller, but greater.
> What would the Third Estate be without the privileged orders? A whole
> by itself, and a prosperous whole.

However, by abolishing the medieval class system of the Estates
the revolutionaries were aiming only at abolishing the link between
class and birth; they were intent only on replacing a class system
which no longer reflected the social reality of economic mobility.

In place of the rigid hereditary orders the revolution substituted
instead a fluid and rational system of economic classes that allowed
the poor to move up to the level of the wealthy and destitute lords
to fall to the bottom of society rather than being artificially sus-
tained in its upper echelons merely because of their ancestors.

The revolutionary bourgeoisie had no intention of abolishing
private property (and thus turning universal citizenship into a truly
universal and equal humanity). They were alarmed that the example of their revolution might provoke demands for full-scale communism. So as an expedient measure they established a spurious
distinction between 'active' and 'passive' citizenship which meant
that, though everyone was equal in civil rights, only the wealthiest
15 per cent of the population (the new 'middle class') were at first
allowed to vote. Instead of making everyone socially equal they
pretended (and are still pretending) to achieve the ideological and
unattainable goal of making everyone middle class, to replace feu-

dal hierarchy with an impossible democracy of universal private-property ownership.

For this reason the revolutionary concept of the nation not only aimed to make universal the free citizenship of the medieval town, it also aimed to make universal the policing function of the medieval town authorities (the guilds and watchmen) who had guaranteed the protection of property, goods and market trade. The nation was to be defined as that area within which the protection and regulation of private-property ownership and free trade could be practically guaranteed by the state. This made the nation a revolutionary idea destined to expand along with the expansion of the bourgeois free market.

Thus the universal citizenship proclaimed by the French revolution benefited the wealthy (indeed established them as the only class able fully to enjoy universal freedom due to their wealth). Class society had been abolished in name only. The revolution merely righted the irrational distortion which kept newly rich citizens away from the levers of power.

In this way the watchword of freedom used during the French revolution, the revolutionary title of 'citizen' applied equally regardless of birth, has come to refer not to a universal humanity as was proclaimed, but exclusively to the emergent beneficiaries of the new fluid class structure, the 'bourgeoisie', citizens who associate freedom with the freedom to buy property (and power) rather than having to inherit it.

Class consciousness

Throughout the eighteenth century many wealthy merchants had bought or married their way into the upper levels of French society in any case. For them the ancient classification of the estates was not a grinding injustice. It could be ignored as a distant and irrelevant feature of history perpetuated only by gossips at the king's court. In day-to-day life many city financiers (Necker included) were scarcely aware of their nominal feudal class positions, having already won the feudal status of 'freemen of the city'.

As the initiators of capitalism, they would have been indignant if reminded that they were officially still classed together with workers and peasants. In reality, for them, economics had replaced birth as the basis of society already.

When the revolution occurred then it did so because even these comfortably assimilated and well-off urban businessmen immediately threw off the decades of social acceptance within feudalism which their financial strength had bought them and angrily acknowledged themselves to be members of the lowest underclass in society, the third estate. They then proceeded to abolish the third estate altogether by dynamically announcing that their hard-won privileged status of freemen was not a privilege at all but one of 'the inalienable rights of man'. In this way the bourgeois revolution developed the basis of revolutionary theory and established the basis for future revolutions towards true equality.

When they declared their 'order consciousness' and extended their solidarity as the revolutionary method of destroying once and for all the feudal order of the third estate, the bourgeoisie unwittingly placed into Pandora's box the means through which we, the remainder of the third estate, can now transcend the capitalist system they ushered in against us.

Their eternal gift to us is a revolutionary consciousness that our class, the working class, can rise up and absorb them, the bourgeoisie, thus abolishing all classes and making humanity finally universal.

**The precocity of revolutionary consciousness: England
1381 and Paris 1871**

Incredibly, the bourgeois consciousness so far described made its
first abortive historical appearance not in enlightenment France
but deep in the gloom of medieval England.

The Peasant's Revolt of 1381 witnessed revolutionary peasants
descending on London in their thousands to dismantle the entire
structure of feudalism. They temporarily destroyed the royal court
and government, executed several ministers and then arranged a
meeting with the boy-king Richard in a London field. Here their
leaders (an embryonic bourgeoisie) requested from him equality
for all before the law and the setting up of a democratic constitution and a capitalist economy. It was a scene which was so in
advance of the capabilities of the feudal world to comprehend let
alone concede to that it still reads as if lifted straight from the
pages of a science-fiction novel.

This rudimentary bourgeois revolution was routed so mercilessly
after it failed that it is tempting to regard history as having tried to
eradicate the evidence of an event from the eighteenth century
which it had inadvertently allowed to erupt in the fourteenth. But
the Peasant's Revolt demonstrates how very early a revolutionary
class can become conscious of its demands (while then addressing
them to figures utterly incapable of understanding them in the
context of the prevailing society).

The four centuries which had to pass before a revolutionary
bourgeoisie were at last successful in overthrowing feudalism is a
salutary reminder that there is nothing inevitable about the abolition of an outmoded class system.

France's successful bourgeois revolution of 1789 meant that progressive consciousness at last achieved enough escape velocity to
begin freeing the world from feudalism. So in similar fashion the
Paris Commune of 1871, 'where the proletariat for the first time

Perpetuating feudalism
helps us develop new crops...

I'M cultivatin
CJD

pass the subsidy, there's a good cha

held political power for two whole months', is our equivalent of the bourgeoisie's premature revolt of 1381.

Marooned in a primitively industrialised city under siege and adrift in a still rural society the consciousness of our revolutionary class, the working class, in 1871 was nevertheless so precocious that we attempted to abolish modern capitalism there at least a century before the bourgeoisie had even managed properly to introduce it!

THE STRUGGLE

Towards abolition of the fluid class system

The modern, fluid class system established by the bourgeois revolution, and present now on a global scale, will only become decrepit like that of its forerunner, the system of the estates, if the economic imperatives that eclipsed genealogy are themselves eclipsed. This will be when humanity's image of itself as a truly universal species becomes the conscious motor of social development. At this point the final separation which regards the imperatives of economic development as existing in phantom opposition to human potentiality (alienation) will be abolished.

Once the fantasy that projects the 'world market' and the 'economy' over us as fake forms of natural phenomena is dispelled we will recognise 'market conditions' for what they are, not prevailing storms but the history-stalling greed of the rich directed against us. This moment is of course a revolutionary one, the point at which the widest imaginable term in economics, 'total world production', becomes the only bourgeois concept still serviceable as a description of our artistic adventure as a newly united human race.

Only the remaining members of the former third estate, now

overwhelmingly made up of us, the world's industrial workers, collectively termed 'the proletariat', can introduce this imperative as our revolutionary project. We are the vast beneficiary class of rising consciousness just as the bourgeoisie has been the beneficiary class of rising economic expectation. We are united on a vast international scale even before we begin to revolt because we are already assembled internationally by the bourgeoisie as the principle ingredient in their world economic system.

For us there is no separation between our work, our lives and our status as an international class and so there is no separation in our consciousness. We seek the culmination of the revolutionary project launched by our class's former allies, the bourgeoisie, to rationalise society and sweep away feudalism. In destroying feudalism the bourgeoisie has merely reproduced a streamlined, rationalised and intensified version of it, an economic system that has accelerated feudalism by stripping it only of genealogical privilege.

Because the conscious project of the poor is yet to succeed, this system is still a class society. Rather than consisting of immutable fixed classes, the society of the bourgeois revolution is one of accelerating class division.

The reproduction of class society

As the bourgeoisie has introduced a fluid class system to the world, each of its members is compelled to pursue the inexorable logic of accumulating more wealth or face tumbling down from the ruling class. The bourgeoisie must behave as competitive capitalists to remain in their class as any successful competitor can replace them.

Capitalism is thus the most efficient means of reproducing class society yet to appear. It is derived from all previous antagonistic class struggles (local, prosaic, diversified and isolated) which, in its attempt to rationalise, centralise, co-ordinate and globalise all features of human society efficiently, it strives to unite within a single, purified struggle between just two global classes, the 'bourgeoisie' and the 'proletariat'. Generated by the continuing existence of private property, these classes are the owners of the means of production and us, their employees.

Capitalism seeks to project our two classes, not merely on a national level, but ultimately across the entire planet, to be administered eventually by a single world government, the institutions of which are currently in formation.

The dominant class in capitalism is the bourgeoisie and it has achieved this position through an historic revolutionary struggle of which its members are justly proud. They are the global rich; their wealth is extracted from us, the world's workers, through their exploitation of us within their global production system.

In absorbing all previous class struggles within itself capitalism also swallows up all previous concepts of liberty and equality which have inspired the struggles of the oppressed against their dominators. But as capitalism is a society of purified and generalised class struggle (rather than being a society that has abolished classes altogether), these concepts are not as yet realised as genuine freedom, democracy and equality in their rational forms but appear only in a modified, partial form.

Capitalism is an hierarchical society of private-property ownership posing as an equal society. The principles of a future society are present within it – democracy, equality and unity – but in a still-alienated form, modified by the principle of private-property ownership. This contradiction drives forward capitalist society.

The making of a global working class

If 'the hand-mill gives you society with the feudal lord: the steam-mill, society with the industrial capitalist', what society does the networked computer give you? A world now dominated by global capitalists and by an increasingly global working class.

The industrial-capitalist system expanded and established itself on a global basis during the twentieth century. Through the flames of two world wars the factory system, with its disciplined work-forces, has been fully established in many areas. The immense pro-ductive forces which have been unleashed have flooded the world with cheap consumer goods and a vertically integrated interna-tional advertising industry to promote both them and the hierar-chical values of the bourgeoisie. As the factory system is linked together across the globe, all its elements are being integrated and rationalised into a single, simultaneous and super-efficient process.

The factory system now extends beyond agriculture and indus-trial manufacturing to cover retail distribution, mass media, finance, accounting and administration, service provision and intellectual production. As it is the networked computer which is making possible this co-ordinating process we can term this pre-sent era of fully linked together capitalism, 'cybernetic capitalism'.

But the super-efficiency of the cybernetic productive system has resulted in a 'realisation' crisis. It has not proved possible for the consumer goods produced to be marketed quickly enough to recoup profits effectively. Despite the networked computer having been harnessed by capitalists in the advanced economic areas so that shops can be linked to warehouses, product lines tracked at point of sale, shelves restocked automatically and poor-selling items identified and withdrawn, too many barriers to the mass-consumption requirements of global capitalism still remain. This is why we are standing on the brink of another gargantuan change in our social organisation.

The networked computer has brought to the fore the urgent need for capitalists to reorganise the physical structure of our soci-eties in order to maximise our consumption of their products.

TWO HUNDRED PHARAOHS.

Chairman Mao has to sell this very book on the streets so he can send his great-grand-daughter to a top English public school. Oh wise Mao!

Having established a factory system for consuming industrial labour time, the ruling classes must now bring fully within the factory system the distribution and retailing of the goods thus produced. This is leading to a general movement in the advanced economic areas towards the 'real subsumption of leisure under capital'.

The capitalists are attempting to seal-off hermetically our leisure time and space and lock us into super-consumption, to regiment leisure time as effectively as labour time, indeed to combine both into a single revalorising act of production and profit. The response we must organise against this movement is the re-assembly of a revolutionary workers' movement. There are signs that such a movement is already reviving from its last assault on capitalism in the late 1960s and early 1970s.

Proletarian revolution: France 1968

The spontaneous seizure of France, one of the advanced industrial economies, by revolutionary workers in 1968 is the last high point achieved by a revolutionary working class. Most subsequent revolts and resistance actions across the world have been inspired by it, including those in Britain.

The ruling classes have spent the last three decades trying to reverse the gains made by the international working class as a result of that uprising (even including the pretence that it was carried out solely by their children in the form of a 'student revolution'). Because it failed, they have been partially successful.

Despite the enormous strides forward it achieved, one of the evident weaknesses of the last revolutionary workers' movement was its acceptance of ideological monologues, all of which provide the basis for further hierarchies to emerge to a greater or lesser extent (in other words, for the bourgeois revolution to intensify).

The revolutionary movement of the late 1960s was not sufficiently powerful to sweep away the ruling classes of the 1970s, but it was sufficiently weak to have produced new ones to replace them if it had.

Acceptance of these ideologies was inevitable given the historical period in which the uprising occurred (indeed the 1968 uprising against bourgeois society was also the process of learning how to break free from those ideologies, all of which are means of saving bourgeois society from abolition).

What is notable therefore is that the workers' movement of the 1960s nevertheless did manage to produce a body of revolutionary theory at an international level which broke free of ideology. Workers began to understand that the bourgeoisie remains revolutionary or else it is doomed and that the existing members of the bourgeoisie are constantly challenged for their positions in the ruling class by the middle classes just below them.

Accordingly, the workers unmasked the innumerable Leninist, Maoist and Trotskyist parties which claimed to be revolutionary organisations working on their behalf as being in reality the hierarchical vehicles of these ambitious middle classes jockeying to use their uprising as the springboard for dislodging and replacing the world's existing rulers.

The 1968 revolution remains inspiring as it witnessed tens of millions of workers within an advanced economy (as advanced for its time as that seized by the revolutionary bourgeoisie in 1789) putting themselves momentarily beyond the reach of these disguised bourgeois revolutionaries and forming instead their own genuine revolutionary working-class organisations. The workers voiced their demands, not within the framework of bourgeois political economy – for higher wages or more consumer goods – but for the abolition of class society altogether through the formation of a rank-and-file system of self management over their world.

The need for a new revolutionary movement

The only means of abolishing class society at our disposal is revolution. The bourgeoisie have established that the transformation of modern society takes place through revolution as demonstrated by their own revolutionary victory over the aristocracy and by the era of constant industrial revolution which this victory has ushered in.

In addition to this, our world is unstable because the bourgeoisie expect that political revolutions will be continually launched against them by the middle classes immediately below. They mount regular take-over bids in a fashion akin to the cut-throat competition for seats on a stock exchange. Though self-serving, these revolutions can be spectacular for those of us expected to die in them for the future benefit of a probationary bourgeois member. The nationalist Cuban revolution of 1959, for instance, catapulted a wealthy sugar-plantation-owner's son, Fidel Castro, into the position he occupies today – billionaire and confidante of fellow magnate Ted Turner.

But while established bourgeoisies often admire such revolutionary activity by the middle classes as precocious business practice, even as they use their armies to oppose it, they react with authentic alarm and horror if confronted by any worker who advocates (or merely explores the possibilities of) a proletarian revolution to democratise the use of their new technologies.

Proletarian revolutionaries are isolated at work and ridiculed as mentally ill or condemned as thieves of labour time (their own lives owned as private property by the bosses). On a global scale they are feared as potential catalysts – instead of inevitable phenomena – seeking to destroy the tranquility of modern life by sabotaging production and capitalist progress. This contradicts the harrowing reality of our current, class society. It is in a permanent state of polarising upheaval which spares none of us because:

the bourgeoisie cannot exist without constantly revolutionising the instruments of production, and thereby the relations of production and with them the whole relations of society. [12]

The fact that bourgeois capitalist society's only legitimacy is derived from having permanently overthrown feudalism means that the bourgeoisie must defend their revolution against any further attempt to realise the principles upon which it is ostensibly based: human liberty, unity and equality.

Because the project of human freedom and equality is the announced project of the bourgeois revolution, a project which it is obstructing, the rational, unannounced project of the bourgeois revolution is for it to consummate itself in total revolution by an international working class.

The real struggle of the human race is for the abolition of all classes (the last, prehistoric remnants of our uneven development as a species) so that we can fully utilise our incredible abilities as nature's only consciously technological creatures. Against this fact the bourgeoisie will mount virtually any Canute-like defence.

Bourgeois society is a society in savage denial of its desire to take the revolutionary overthrow of feudalism to its rational conclusion, the conscious unity of the species. Only the assembly of a revolutionary workers' movement can complete the task of liberating humanity and the revival by the current workers' movement of our revolutionary project remains an exhilarating possibility.

The power of the ruling classes to control the oppressed of today's world is potentially weaker than that which has been at the disposal of all previously dominant classes. They are themselves daily making it weaker as they progressively link together the world's poor into a single vast workforce and narrow the choices of

12 Karl Marx and Frederick Engels, *The Communist Manifesto*, 1848

this workforce until we are presented, sooner or later, with just a single choice: effective slavery or revolution.

The poverty of alienation in a world of abundance

The alternative to a revolutionary movement is allowing the terrible costs of everyday life to continue unchallenged under current social conditions.

Despite the colossal productive abilities and endless possibilities of today's industrial technology, which could easily deliver us into a world of plenty within which we could live totally fulfilling and communicative lives, the current reality of its primitive use under capitalism means that we live in a world in which soul-crushing poverty, both absolute and relative, is the experience of most people across both advanced and developing economic areas.

The gulf between rich and poor on both global and national scales is unprecedented. The underlying reality of this material poverty (affecting more than a quarter of the population in industrialised areas[13]) is the poverty of everyday life. Lives that are divorced from purpose and creativity are now lived by the vast bulk of the world's population.

The effects of this alienation are not spiritual but physical and social. Hierarchical control of people's everyday lives makes them physically and mentally ill. Bullying, over-work, depression, self-hatred and boredom – these become the prime causes of stress and stress-related illnesses, some virtually unknown outside the industrialised world.

Compounding the incidence of these chronic conditions are the everyday frustrations of poor-quality sexual and social relation-

---

13 For example; in July 1999 a baby (Leroy Elders) died of malnutrition in Britain despite it being a g7 economy nation. His parents could not afford proper baby-food.

ships, low self-esteem being the most common cause of aggression, domestic abuse and street violence, loneliness and isolation. These in turn generate commonplace eating disorders and nicotine, alcohol and drug addiction. Pollution, concentrated in industrialised working-class areas, causes widespread immune- and respiratory-system illnesses.

These are just some of the life-debasing, and frequently fatal, manifestations of the intense alienation required by advanced capitalism. In developing countries the inverse effects of alienation are experienced: famine, malnutrition and poor healthcare drive peasants into the slums of urban sprawl where the misery of life under backward capitalism awaits them.

> Among the 4.4 billion people in developing countries, almost three-fifths (over half the world's population) lack basic sanitation, one-third have no safe drinking water, one-quarter have inadequate housing, while one-fifth are undernourished and the same proportion have no access to modern health care.[14]

Monopoly and surplus

The very basis of capitalist society is its aim to monopolise our environment so as to close off access to any alternative methods of surviving independently of the profit system it operates. Once we have been driven into cities we must all apply to the bosses for work within their factories and offices in order to survive.

Capitalism's factory system can be viewed as a vast machine for exploiting us. Not only are we compelled to work within it but in reality we are paid virtually nothing for doing so. Profits are derived from the 'surplus labour' which is rinsed out of us every day.

14 *United Nations Human Development Report,* 1998.

Because they control our working environment, the rich are able to make us work longer than we actually need to in order to replace the wear and tear of the materials we use up in production (including the costs of feeding and housing ourselves, costs deducted by the rich from our wages after work). But our species now possesses industrial equipment which is so hyper-efficient that, as part of a global system, it will have already 'earned us back our daily living' (as well as having replaced the cost of everything used up) almost within seconds of it being switched on. The rest of our time at work we spend churning out wealth that will never appear in our wages.

> Capital therefore is not just the command over labour, it is essentially the command over unpaid labour. All surplus-value, whatever particular form (profit, interest or rent) it may subsequently crystallise into, is in substance the materialisation of unpaid, 'alien' labour-time ... the unpaid labour of other people.[15]

This is the source of the oceanic assets of today's billionaires. The monopoly system, through interest, rent, mortgage payments, shares and bonds, ensures it filters up into their pockets. The power that this 'surplus value' concentrates in the hands of the global rich and allows them to wield over our world is awesome. The technology which, if directed by us, could transform this world into a paradise on earth, is instead used to construct the imbecilic environment conjured up by the immensely rich against us.

Monopoly capitalist society

Monopoly capitalism lays waste to developing areas with intensive mining, farming and population resettlement policies in the fields of production as well as brutal control over the distribution of

15 Karl Marx, *Capital*, 1867.

In 1991 the Duke of Westminster decides that all elected politicians are Bolsheviks.

pharmaceuticals, food and information. Under monopoly conditions in all areas of the world, culture becomes industrialised and imposed from above by a hierarchical system of distribution.

The mass media, television, the opinions of newspapers and the topics of television programmes, pop songs and software, all these are owned and obliquely controlled by an ever-diminishing bourgeois clique. At the highest levels (at least during inaugural phases) their mass media are managed for them predominantly by upper-class men (and a very few women), often with military backgrounds. The terms of reference for the topics of everyday conversation and communication are therefore set for the world's public by a small group of ruling-class operators, their managerial sympathisers and their allies in the military, civil services and police, and disseminated across all nations.

Though the resultant content is a vast, ephemeral tapioca of non-threatening inanity and an endless research project into the 'glamour' and controversy of the middle classes, the ludicrous whims and prejudices of a few hundred billionaires are also forced upon us as a significant element of our global culture. Though these are principally the urgent needs of their business interests (the 'need' for regressive taxes, low wages and anti-communism), such is their inability to conceive of progress as involving the whole human race that their cultural contributions reflect instead the infantile panic that their egos will not survive beyond their own deaths.

As a result, they may actually arrange for the cryogenic preservation of their bodies in private while sponsoring the world's religions which promise them that hierarchy can continue even after death. In despair they erect pathetically grandiose monuments (which have reached levels of banality as intense as attempting to set a hot-air ballooning record) which have little or no relevance to the world's general population but which they hope will give them a form of immortality.

Because the world's media dotes on the private fears and bigotries of an economically invincible but socially retarded set of billionaires, a constant litany of crime figures, sexist, racist and nationalist imagery[16] and trivia reduces the quality of human communication. An increasing number of media techniques are used to disguise this monologue as pseudo-dialogue (at their simplest, the invented personalisation of impassioned editorials and speech to camera; at the most sophisticated, television chat-shows, studio discussions, documentaries, newspaper questionnaires and 'phone polls, etc.). The move towards monopoly vastly accelerated during the 1980s and 1990s, with today's global corporations grown out of state control now dwarfing the cartels, combines and 'zaibatsus' of the last era of aggressive, private monopoly capitalism in the 1930s.

The welfare state internationalised

If the executive institutions of the nation state in the nineteenth century were 'but a committee for managing the common affairs of the whole bourgeoisie',[17] then it takes global institutions to fulfil that role for the rich of today.

The rich have erected, through the co-ordinated efforts of their governments, a system of regressive tax exemption across the world. This substitutes taxes on wealth by taxes on consumption and mimics the tax system employed by the pre-revolutionary French monarchy in its terminal phase. It forces the poorest to

16 This nationalist imagery is hierarchical as well, designed to encourage each
    nation's workers to isolate ourselves from neighbouring workforces by identifying
    with our local bourgeois nation. But beyond this we are encouraged to identify
    with the power of the leading economies and ultimately with the global values of
    'Hollywood nationalism'.

17 *The Communist Manifesto.*

work hardest, generating stupendous stockpiles of surplus value for the ruling class. The rich are therefore driving us towards a situation where a global fiscal crisis could facilitate a technical French revolution at a planetary level.

This would not be the proletarian revolution we so desperately require but some unimaginably monstrous 'world bourgeois revolution', lead against us on the bourgeoisie's behalf by the 'radical' middle classes. It would enable those who emerged unscathed to establish a world government to legalise their global domination.

In the meantime the rich are making do with internationalising the state mechanism they developed to protect capitalism from its internal problems in the last century, the 'welfare state' (the state redefined as a vast insurance company for the rich masquerading as a welfare agency for all).

As soon as industrial capitalism had grown sufficiently large to be recognised as an on-going system (owned by the rich) rather than just a collective term for factory owners, it was recognised that this system was prone to attack from below and to collapse from above. The state was therefore expanded to take over the management and welfare of the capitalist system (mystically christened 'the economy') on behalf of the rich as a class.

Welfare arose within industrial societies from the late 1800s as a nation-by-nation means of alleviating the contradictions of large-scale private-property ownership (that is, planning to protect capitalism from the wrath of its workers and the chaos of its markets). Welfare was introduced in Britain in its modern form in 1919 when the Lloyd George government set up a range of state-run insurance schemes. Following the example set by Bismarck, these included rudimentary protection against unemployment and old age in order to prevent social hardship from becoming a rallying point for revolutionary action by the industrial working class. But the largest single part of this scheme was the 'Export Credit Guarantee', an insurance scheme protecting British exporters against bad debts they might incur as a result of foreign revolutions (prompted of course by the Russian revolution).

An apologetic admission by the British Empire to its capitalists, that the revolutionary actions of other country's workers were beyond its control, the scheme obviously carried within it the implied promise to eventually bring all the world's workers within the control of the leading bourgeois states by establishing global institutions.

And today this promise is being fulfilled. The welfare state has duly matured and become titanically powerful. It has broken free from its national moorings to overarch the capitalist world as today's global economic planning system, economic intervention on a scale undreamt of even as recently as the 1960s. Welfare spending has increased exponentially in every major nation and has been increasingly targeted towards its true purpose, subsidising and protecting the rich.

The welfare state now consists primarily of a plethora of international monetary organisations, the IMF, G7, World Trade Organisation, etc., all in effect aggrandised insurance schemes that the leading nations have pooled together to create to protect their exporters against the unpredictable actions of the world's workers. These institutions, and many others, are rapidly merging into a single Grand Prix touring economic summit, held in almost permanent session.

The protection and welfare of the world capitalist system has replaced every other ideological justification for state control. Even Beijing's bureaucrats are now taking their seats alongside other capitalist planners in seeking to stabilise world markets. Ensuring that exporters get paid and revolutions do not cancel out profits is leading to the creation of a world police force for markets and populations.

War

Ultimately underpinning the early welfare state of the leading industrial nations was the belief that overseas markets must be conquered and colonised in order to extend capitalism (and to prevent asset-seizing revolutions). The international welfare state now emerging seeks to plan the co-ordinated conquest and colonisation of the entire world as a single market (the colonisation of everyday life) and prevent an asset-seizing revolution occurring at the global level. This would be the world proletarian revolution the ultra-wealthy know to be a possibility because it has already been theorised by the workers' movement as our supreme goal. The ultimate method of insuring capitalism is to break all revolutionary workers' movements using war. Nothing can better guarantee high profits, low wages and the reimbursement of exporters for decades afterwards.

As early as 1790 employers were voicing their war manifesto as the antidote to revolutionary activity by their employees:

'There wants a war to reduce wages', was the cry of some northern gentry in the 1790s.[18]

By the first decade of the twentieth century this cry had become open hysteria. Because, despite the weaknesses of infancy, the workers' movement managed to orchestrate an escalating wave of general strikes across Europe and America between 1903 and 1914. The bosses' reaction was to plan with their erstwhile enemies, the aristocracy, the first fratricidal European war designed to bury tens of thousands of rebellious employees in trenches.

The revolutionary crisis of 1913–14 (which saw Britain on the brink of a general strike and Europe swept by factory occupations)

18 *The Making of the English Working Class.*

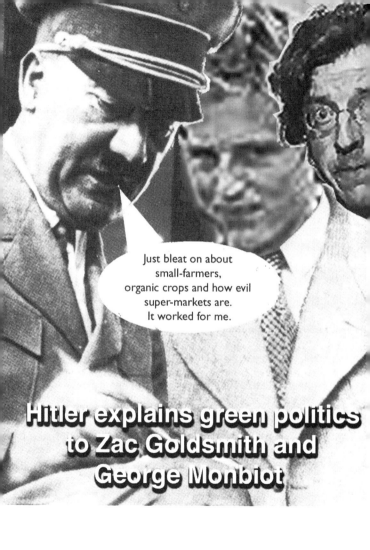

prompted the bosses to fire the starting pistol for their first 'Great War' against the working class. Overnight Europe's governments made simultaneous declarations of war on each other in order to wrong-foot revolutionary labour. This utterly contrived conflict was used to impose states of emergency in all factories, extending working hours and reducing safety. Meanwhile the ultimate unsafe workplace, the battlefield, hung ominously over the head of every worker not already at 'the front'. The Great War also established the concept of the 'home front', the crude sucking of home life and leisure time into the maw of universal factory production for the first time.

War is bullying on a awesome scale. It cows us into submission and breaks our international unity. War enables the ruling class to establish an environment conducive to intensifying their industrialism, flame-testing experimental production and organisational techniques.

But though wars initially smash revolutionary workers' movements and prepare the ground for new production methods, they also unleash vast and dangerously unpredictable consequences. If wars are capitalism's means of facilitating its advance as a system by leaps and bounds, they carry within them the possibility that they will go out of control and become the means of facilitating an advance beyond the capitalist system altogether.

The pre-war revolutionary movements of the workers may, through wartime organisation and struggle, come to be raised up into armed revolutionary struggle on an international scale. The chance given to capitalists by war to introduce a more advanced production system may lead, inadvertently, to the superseding of capitalism altogether.

With this danger in mind, the burgeoning global welfare system will soon seek to plan the suppression of workers in advance of a rise in our militancy rather than convening a world war in order to break us after we have had time to form a revolt. The temporary drafting of the American workforce in 1946 to prevent a general strike in the USA was a crude early emergence of this tendency of the global welfare state[19] (a tendency ultimately doomed to create world government and thus undermine itself. For once implemented global class consciousness will arise in reaction to such centralised capital).

Militarism and labour discipline

War was ameliorated in advanced economic areas in the latter half of the twentieth century because labour discipline had been successfully enforced. Early capitalist factory owners were constantly dismayed at the endemic absenteeism of their workers. Without warning, they would quit their factories and cities and return to peasant villages at harvest-time, or after having accumulated enough money from factory work, or when they decided to travel.

These temporary and seasonal workers plagued early British industry as they were to plague early Soviet planners, American car-factory owners and many others. The process of dinning into workers' heads the understanding that factory work was a permanent condition of continuous shifts became the general struggle against the peasantry which characterises the development of industrial societies.

This struggle was accelerated in the gigantic industrialised wars of the twentieth century in the advanced economic areas. These

19 In May 1946, in the face of a rapidly spreading general strike in the United States, PresidentTruman requested, and was granted, 'temporary, emergency legislation to draft into the Army all workers striking against the government'. This legislation was later overturned by the Senate as unconstitutional but had by then achieved its aim.

wars created regimented labour-forces and treated absenteeism with martial law. New wars can therefore be expected in the so-called developing nations, if labour discipline there is not successfully imposed upon these predominantly peasant economies by the pressure of the world market alone.

In the advanced economic areas it is the regimentation of leisure time which is now more important. It is not possible to predict what kind of social warfare will be employed to enforce 'leisure discipline' on the West's workers.

For the time being bourgeois global planning is content cynically to bombard sparsely populated countries as theatrical wars to intimidate European and American workforces. Murderous pantomimes such as the Libya crisis of 1986 sometimes have economic purposes, acting as giant trade fairs for market-testing new weapons, pharmaceuticals and management techniques. More frequently they coincide with rising worker discontent in the major economies. Theatrical wars are both distractions and subliminal disciplinaries for the West's workers. In this way they are identical to the public chasing and capture of supermarket shoplifters by security guards, performances put on as much to intimidate shoppers as to catch the shoplifter.

Our revolutionary project revives

Despite the attempts of the world's bourgeoisie to head off worker militancy, their watchdogs, the global trades-union bosses, early on publicly warned them that a revolutionary proletariat is again beginning to form.[20] After decades of repression we have begun to

20 In 1994 John Monks of Britain's TUC warned European bosses that workforces were becoming militant again for the first time since the 1970s.

assemble for a fresh attempt at seizing history. An irresistible dialectic is building between the Cyclopean possibilities of the bourgeoisie's new high technology and the powerful rise in proletarian consciousness brought about by the concomitant dissolution of Stalinism.

The illusion that the Soviet Union was an opposing force to the capitalist West mesmerised a generation of workers on both sides of the Berlin Wall. This illusion is now shattered.

In China an unprecedented migration from countryside to the cities has taken place since 1990 so that today, as never before in history, the working class forms a massive segment of the world's population, almost half of humanity. The possibility of total proletarian revolution is therefore greater than ever before.

Germany's careful owner Johanna Quandt dreams that she is a Messiah for cars

US

Solidarity

The fact that social class continues to divide the human race indicates that, after forty thousand years, our species is still only in the prehistoric phase of development. But today's class struggle is global, intense and dynamic.

The contest is not just between a revolutionary movement and its local oppressors – as has always been the case before – it is now between two immense classes, both of which are revolutionary and each of which seeks to accomplish a worldwide revolution against the other. This at last makes possible the mission of the human race as a whole because we are nature's only revolutionary species.

Our global class struggle is in fact our breathtaking attempt to become conscious of our mission to free ourselves of all divisions and to unify so that we can at last wield our awesome, supernatural powers together. Unique amongst all the creatures on earth, we are self-conscious and once we are able to experience this self-consciousness not just as individuals but as a species we will be able collectively to foretell our futures by planning them in advance.

However, this unification process cannot take place within the partial conditions of the bourgeoisie's revolution. That revolution will only ever be able to centralise humanity up to the point of a single world government or global currency union, either of which would merely intensify our class struggle. We can only unite if we abolish all classes.

Because it is simultaneously the last prehistoric class of oppressors and the first-ever class of successful revolutionaries, the bourgeoisie represents the earliest appearance of the revolutionary consciousness we will require to achieve this aim.

The bourgeois revolution and its capitalist economy uphold the unprecedented ideals of liberty and equality of opportunity for each person. These historically unique ideals provide the basis for a world of freely associating individuals to be brought into being, a world of individuals freed from the social handicap of class division and able to recognise themselves as members of a united species.

The centralising effect of the capitalist economy worldwide brings almost the whole of the human race together in unconscious cooperation already, but only in order for us to act as a single gigantic workforce for the rich. Having established that the mass cooperation of the human race is possible, the bourgeois revolution itself must now be overthrown by us in order to realise this cooperation as the total freedom of human solidarity.

The proletariat: a global industrial working class

The historical mission of the workers' movement is to establish a consciousness of ourselves as a single class whose goal is to embody the whole of humanity through the abolition of all classes.

The first step taken by the workers' movement to achieve this is to make us all aware that we are members of an international working class or 'proletariat'. These are terms used to describe the final class in human history, the class containing all industrial workers.

The proletariat is the industrialisation of the Third Estate, a class now comprising almost half of the entire population of the world.

Instead of being a mass of peasants still able to eke out an existence on a tiny plot of land, it now consists of us, the industrial workers who can only provide for ourselves by selling our labour to the owners of the factory system, the bourgeoisie (or by relying on various doles provided by them). For this reason our regard for our own self-interest as a class is synonymous with our humanity, for only the revolutionary overthrow of class society will end our alienation (and so that of humanity itself).

As the working class, we therefore recognise ourselves as revolutionary or we are nothing but inert ingredients in factory production, like so many bales of steel. The factory system is the system of industrialised production and distribution owned by the bourgeoisie which uses applied science to extract surplus value from us on the largest possible scale (to rob us of our lives).

Factory work (i.e. regimented labour), more frequently referred to simply as 'work' because it encompasses most forms of employment from retail and services to administration and not merely manufacturing, is the source of profit for the rich. It is experienced by us, the working class, as a system of hierarchical instructions (our 'duties'), the purpose of which we are permitted no democratic control over nor creative input beyond strict parameters.

The enormous productive possibilities of our work are wasted. They are channelled towards benefiting the bourgeoisie rather than all of us and then only in the primitive and wasteful economic form of profits (our stolen labour-time).

The revolutionary proletariat can therefore expand upon the earlier revolutionary manifesto of the bourgeoisie by asking:

What is the Proletariat? – All of Humanity.
What have we been in capitalist society up till now? -- Nothing but an

ingredient in the bourgeoisie's production process.

What do we desire to be? Conscious.

Take away the rest of the class system and we become free,
a whole species, liberated from prehistoric conditions and arrived at the
true beginning of history at last.

As consumers

Aware of the creative freedom its existence is holding back, capitalism temporarily raises a phantom version of human liberation
when it starts to address us as prospective consumers. As the workers' movement of the 1960s observed:

> whereas in the primitive stage of capitalist accumulation 'political
> economy treats the proletarian as a mere worker' who must receive only
> the minimum necessary to guarantee his labour-power, and never
> considers him 'in his leisure, in his humanity,' these ideas of the ruling
> class are revised just as soon as so great an abundance of commodities
> begins to be produced that a surplus 'collaboration' is required of workers.
> All of a sudden the workers discover that they are no longer invariably
> subject to the total contempt so clearly built into every aspect of the
> organisation and management of production; instead they find that every
> day, once work is over, they are treated like grown-ups, with a great show
> of solicitude and politeness, in their new role as consumers.[21]

Of course this new 'solicitude and politeness' is merely an illegible
photocopy of the original. It is taken from the genuine respect
accorded by the ruling class to itself.

As the ruling class is the only real 'leisure class', its humanity for
itself derives from its position as society's ultimate class of con-

21 *The Society of the Spectacle.*

sumers, those able to afford the ultimate, self-replenishing luxury of consuming human lives (consuming the stolen labour time of factory workers). However, capitalism constantly strives towards bringing working-class leisure and consumption within the regimentation it has already established for our labour. Once successful, its pseudo-'humanity' towards us as shoppers will wilt back to the level of the 'humanity' already expressed towards us as workers.

The proletarian pseudo-middle class

While senior managers are confirmed members of the world's middle classes, junior managers and technicians are contentious members of the industrial proletariat forming a 'pseudo-middle class' at work.

From capitalism's viewpoint anyone standing outside the proletarianisation process who is not an owner of the means of production is an historical anomaly.

Factories can take any shape or form and any form of productive activity can become industrialised within them. So the logic of the factory system ensures that these 'living fly-wheels for correcting capitalist machinery', the workers who erroneously believe themselves to be 'middle class' because of petty positions of power or knowledge, are increasingly 'proletarianised'.

Because they are entrusted by the bosses to look after the technology and personnel of the workplace (i.e. 'are enlisted in the service of capital to be functionally dominant over the workers'), the self-deluding pseudo-middle classes at work often identify themselves with the bosses who secretly despise them and research ways of by-passing the need for their existence.

The 'new intelligentsia' [can be] used as a term to describe these engineers and technicians employed in the installation, operation, supervision and

servicing of large-scale modern plants and their comprehensively
rationalised labour-processes … These mere managerial employees, by no
means particularly highly paid, [can often] seem passionately committed
to the interests of capital without having any personal shares in its
winnings [because] in the hierarchical organisation of mass-production
they occupy a position which is specific and profiled enough to possess
the semblance of class character.[22]

But this 'class character' is an illusion. The proletariat which these
middle-class human-resource managers and technicians fondly
imagine they have risen above is constantly 'rising up' further to
engulf them again. They too lose all creative input into their labour
and find that their work (the management of workers or the maintenance of advanced production systems) is increasingly broken
down into parcels of mindless repetitive tasks. It is the networked
computer which is currently assisting in this.

A pseudo-middle class of the professionals, skilled workers and
dictatorial line-managers required to enforce the factory system on
unskilled workers will always form the flotsam on the surface of
any wave of technological innovation. But each successive wave
engulfs this ephemeral class to a greater degree because each further absorbs into its physical structure and operation the functions
of skilled labour and the dictatorial powers of line-management.

Each wave of new technology confronts us ever more profoundly as having anticipated within itself any skills required for its
operation and as being itself our manager. Put frankly, each new
wave of technology throws up a more efficient method of proletarianisation by diminishing the need for a technical middle class and
by industrialising their managerial tasks (which they may still perform but as proletarians).

22 Alfred Sohn-Rethel, *The Economy and Class Structure of German Fascism*, 1978.

The peasantry

The greatest remaining non-proletarianised section of the human race is the peasantry. Peasants are tenant-farmers who rent their small-holdings and sell their surplus food on the open market. They currently represent a fraction under 50 per cent of the world's population. Large-scale landowners or industrialists exploit the peasantry on their lands by fixing rents or mortgages at high levels or rigging the markets for farm produce.

Once industrialisation has begun to revolutionise agriculture, pressures arise to abolish the patchwork villages of the peasantry and replace them with the gigantic fields of factory farming. Peasants are driven off the land and into the cities. But despite the revolutionary peasant movements which this economic pressure generates, each revolutionary workers' movement prematurely announces the disappearance of the peasantry in our eagerness for a world where only proletarians and bourgeoisie face each other for a final struggle.

This is because, paradoxically, peasants thwart social revolution when they take revolutionary action. Unlike proletarians, peasants are not forced to confront totality when they act as revolutionaries.

If as proletarians we set out to 'seize the means of production', we immediately find ourselves engaged in trying to dispossess the bourgeoisie of its entire capitalist system. As capitalism is interlinked across the world, this rapidly forces upon us the realisation that our revolution has no feasible choice or realistic goal but to try and engage all workers in seizing the entire world and thus in abolishing capitalism and with it class society.

When peasants seize their means of production, on the other hand, their social revolution comes to an abrupt halt right at their feet. With their seizure of land (usually made possible by revolutionary workers miles away in the cities having obligingly put their absentee landlords to flight) peasants transform rural society into an isolated patchwork of independent small farm-holdings. Post-revolutionary peasants then attempt to establish a bucolic, localised and stagnant free-market economy until the bourgeois revolution reaches into this horrifying glaciation of history to proletarianise the peasants by force. And, in fact, the disappearance of the peasantry was a steady phenomenon of the twentieth century, one marked by levels of brutality beyond anything ever witnessed by the human race before.

As the bourgeois revolution has accelerated, peasants, revolutionary or otherwise, have suffered increasingly in its wake. Most of course have been forced to leave their peasant nature at the city border. Capitalism has specialised above all else in reaching into the fields, deserts, forests and jungles and sucking the world's remaining peasants and hunter-gatherers into the gaping maws of urban shanty-towns.

But capitalism's brutal need to quickly convert rural peasants into urban proletarians has required it to cow them with terror wherever they have attempted to stay on the land. If the early dispossession process of English enclosure which first forced peasants into the towns in the sixteenth century was 'written in blood and flames', then these flames were mere sparks by comparison to those that accompanied the 'clearing of the estates' in Scotland, Ireland, and north America during the nineteenth century.

And as capitalism has rippled outwards from northern Europe so its blood-lust has increased exponentially. In Russia, eastern Europe, south and central America, Africa and south-east Asia, the clearing of the estates took on its industrialised form in the twentieth century as genocide. Simultaneously, the slow extinction of British home-working artisans, who attempted futilely to compete with the output of the new industrial factories of the 1800s, expanded to become a purge of home-workers across the entire globe during the following century.

Capitalism proceeds by alienating humanity. This is its secret. The destruction of the world's peasantry is not carried out due to some ideological hatred of peasants by the world's capitalists. Nor are peasants somehow inferior human beings who have out-lived their historical usefulness.

The aim of capitalist accumulation is not to eradicate peasants *per se* but to make alienation universal and intense. In order to realise this aim, capitalism must separate all human beings from independent existence, force us increasingly to rely on the consumption of manufactured goods for our survival, and above all give us no alternative but to seek work in the factory system in order to obtain wages to buy these goods. Peasants must have any semblance of their world taken away from them and sold back to them as the alien environment of the city.

Far from hating peasants, the bourgeois class is keen to preserve peasant awe and loyalty to landlords and emperors while transferring it on to itself, in the form of loyalty to the bourgeois state and eventually as loyalty to bourgeoisie-owned companies. But to do this the bourgeoisie must triumph in their struggle with the aristocracy in order to establish the bourgeois state.

So profound is this struggle that it engages the whole of the population in social revolution and is therefore carried out on the only revolutionary terrain on which all objectified classes can temporarily unite, humanity's struggle against its alienation.

In their need to enlist peasants and urban workers in the revolutionary struggle, the bourgeoisie promise to end exploitation by the aristocracy and establish democracy, but their commitment to democracy is only a commitment to democratise exploitation, to broaden the class of exploiters from a group of aristocratic families outwards to cover a fluid class, the bourgeoisie.

Fidel Castro dreams of buying investment property in Stoke Newington

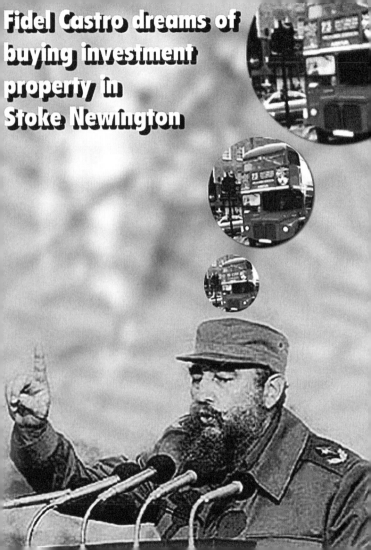

THE STALEMATE

Revolutionary bourgeoisie in the 20th century

The primary example of a peasantry-dissolving bourgeois revolution in the twentieth century can be found in the aftermath of the Russian revolution of 1917. Following on from the earlier revolution of 1905 (which witnessed the formation of workers councils or 'soviets' for the first time by Russia's minute working class), the 1917 uprising was the first to be initiated by a revolutionary proletariat.

An urban working class, the primary product of industrial capitalism, had, incongruously, emerged within a still-feudal state. The embryonic proletarian revolution it launched represented the maturing of the one whose birth-pangs had been witnessed at the Paris Commune in 1871 when a city was briefly made classless for the first time in history.

But the Russian revolution was a titanic contradiction. A minute urban working class had led a revolution against industrial capitalism from within a still over-whelmingly rural and feudal society. So acute was this disjunction that it triggered the formation of a new type of bourgeoisie specifically equipped to seize control of this phenomenon and harness it.

Unlike feudal society, bourgeois society is revolutionary. Once victorious the bourgeoisie remains revolutionary or else it is replaced by new, more dynamic members. And this fate befalls any feudal relic attempting to pose as a member of this new class even more swiftly.

Although a feudal king may allow modern factory equipment to be imported from the advanced areas where the bourgeoisie has already triumphed, paradoxically the aristocratic factory owners who then pose as a bourgeoisie cannot produce their own bourgeois revolution. Capitalism cannot be grafted on to the stagnation of feudal society and be made to develop at the seasonal pace of feudalism.

Instead, planted like a demon-seed, advanced industrial capitalism tears feudalism apart from the womb outwards. It immediately generates from within itself the real classes it requires to revolutionise society as well as production, a proletariat and a class of dynamic would-be owners distinct from any group of feudal aristocrats who have already imported the factory system piecemeal and attempted to tend it like one of their country estates. This dynamic class which industrial capitalism requires is not simply a bourgeoisie but a revolutionary bourgeoisie, like that which seized France in 1789.

Marxist bourgeoisies

Where a bourgeois underclass found itself still struggling with feudalism during the twentieth century, it seized its slogans directly from the workers. These industrial workers had been created by an imported factory system it was normally charged with introducing itself. This rhetoric was merged with the most advanced form of its own science, political economy, wherever it needed to justify itself as an emergency programme in backward areas.

Inevitably named after the workers' own scientist, 'Marxism' is an ideology of emergency state planning to introduce factories allegedly in the name of their workers. It was fashioned by the first revolutionary bourgeois underclass that had to contend with (and accommodate) a small but already militant proletariat which had problematically come into existence before its victory.

The ideology of Marxism thus played the same role in the twentieth century as the ideology of revolutionary liberalism did during the early stage of capitalism, but this time raised to an industrial level. In other words, Marxism was industrialised liberalism. It offered total freedom – as long as that freedon was controlled by an elite.

Despite this industrialisation of theory the entire world did not need to become 'Marxist' during the twentieth century. The capitalist system only needed to justify itself in those areas where an embryonic bourgeoisie was still in the process of overthrowing a feudal aristocracy who had prematurely created, through imported technology, an industrial workforce now precociously preempting them with a proletarian revolution of its own.

Marxism was needed where obedience to the factory system was yet to be established. Industrialising governments in economically backward areas needed to ensure worker acceptance for the introduction of a factory system under their control during the twentieth century. They did so by presenting the imposition of the factory system as a popular revolution, claiming it continued the genuine revolutionary seizure of factories by the early workers' movement.

Proletarianised bourgeois revolution: Russia 1917

Thus the class that seized control of the Russian revolution of 1917 was not the factory-owning aristocracy of Moscow and St Petersburg. These aristocrats only advertised the need for a revolutionary bourgeoisie to replace them. First they toyed with importing factories, then they acted out a charade when they partially supported the workers' uprising of 1905. Instead it was a revolutionary movement drawn from the frustrated middle classes, the embryonic bourgeoisie assembled in the Bolshevik Party.

After many failed attempts by revolutionary bourgeois movements to catapult Russia out of feudalism (the Nihilists, Narodniks, etc.), the Bolsheviks at last succeeded. They did so by seizing the larval proletarian revolution and imposing their party structure on it. Thus they demonstrated that bourgeois revolution is 'bottom-feeding', it manifests and rejuvenates itself by elevating to power only those 'extreme' political groups or entrepreneurs, no matter how minor, who can align themselves so closely with the demands of the revolutionary situation (whether technological or social) that that situation comes to be identified with the pre-established hierarchical structure of their own organisations.

This in fact is the true definition of a revolutionary bourgeois, someone who successfully reinterprets the revolution of the masses, and the potential of new technology, hierarchically.

The Bolsheviks' slogans distinguished them as the genuine face of bourgeois revolution in Russia. Unlike the paternalist aristocratic factory owners who supported a reformed monarchy, the Bolsheviks (like the revolutionaries of 1789) called for universal freedom and equality and merged themselves with the struggle of the masses in order to seize hold of it.

Their slogans were intensified versions of those used in 1789. Instead of parliamentary democracy, the Bolsheviks claimed to endorse the direct democracy of workers councils (and to embody it during the October revolution). This was the industrialised form of intense democracy being explored in the first faltering steps of the revolutionary working class.

The massive expansion of the bourgeois world market by 1917 provoked the tiny Russian proletariat to call for total, global freedom during their uprising. The Bolsheviks had no choice but to appropriate this audacious programme and in their early rhetoric (temporarily) redefine the 'national revolution' they sought to introduce as a 'world revolution'.

But although bourgeoisies invariably lead the charge of social revolutions in the name of freedom and democracy, it is not possible for them actually to allow democratic governments (either parliamentary or proletarian) to spring from the shadows of feudal decline. Democracy must be postponed until it can be a democracy that guarantees the security of bourgeois investments – the private property and factory system which first have to be properly established.

Bolshevism

For this reason the post-revolutionary Constituent Assembly of Russia was effectively suspended for 75 years, being replaced by Bolshevik dictatorship within a month of its first elections. From its seizure of power onwards, the victorious Bolshevik Party began to spawn a bewildering array of supposedly rival doctrines, each named after ministers in its original government and each allegedly denoting an alternative course which their revolution ought to have taken. Some of these doctrines still exist today, known variously as 'Leninism', 'Trotskyism' and 'Stalinism'. In reality though, these were not separate doctrines at all but grandiose terms for the inevitable phases the Bolsheviks' bourgeois revolution had to go through if it was to modernise Russia and defeat her small but precociously revolutionary working class for the eventual benefit of international capitalism.

A clue to the bourgeois priorities of Bolshevism can be gleaned from the memoirs of the American capitalist Armand Hammer, an early visitor to the Soviet Republic in search of bargains. He described the asbestos mining concessions he was offered by Lenin in the following terms:

> I felt almost as if I had been taken up to the top of a mountain from which all Russia could be seen below and Lenin had said, 'Take your pick'. This immense country, with its inestimable wealth of natural resources, its vast reserves of labour and its almost untouched potential, had been laid open to me by its leader.. With Lenin's protection and patronage I could add an incalculable fortune to my present wealth …

When Hammer was then told to ask security minister Trotsky for guards to protect his new Russian investments Trotsky informed him that:

> he had just returned from an inspection trip through the Urals and was convinced that it offered great possibilities to American capital. He asked whether the financial circles of the United States regarded Russia as a desirable field of investment and felt that they ought to because as Russia had had its Revolution, capital was really safer there than anywhere else.[23]

Desperate to import Western start-up technology and capital to their backward feudal state, the Bolsheviks maintained an open-door policy to Western industrialists. In this period Trotsky was most eager to export the Bolshevik revolution in return for supplies – in practice this meant encouraging Western industrialists to view Bolshevism as a super-efficient business partner. For instance, when agreeing to send his technicians to Russia to help set up Taylorised tractor-assembly lines, the American car magnate Henry

23 Armand Hammer, *Hammer: Witness to History*, 1987 .

Ford approved of the fact that 'the Bolsheviks were starting from the ground up and trying to jump right away from the late Middle Ages to the twentieth century'.[24]

Once enough modern technology had been imported and installed for Russia to attempt to rival the West's production, the Bolsheviks quickly closed their open door. In the name of national pride they concentrated instead upon the other half of their modernising equation, the terrorising of their own workforce to generate enough factory goods and surplus value to send abroad. Leninism and Trotskyism were therefore the expansionist periods of Stalinism just as Stalinism was later to become the protectionist period of Trotskyism.

Stalinism

Stalinism is the name for mature Bolshevism. It was the means, under emergency conditions, of dispelling feudal property relations and establishing factory labour within a still-peasant-dominated society, specifically because this society had pioneered a workers' revolution in its cities due to the existence of an external capitalist world from which factories had already been imported.

Stalinism stabilised the minute Russian proletarian revolution by first swamping it with the much greater effects of the peasant revolution in the countryside and then turning it into a new type of bourgeois revolution, one which brazenly fashioned for itself a false proletarian image (rather than a false liberal one as had been used in France). This was because it followed the industrial revolution of the nineteenth century and therefore the appearance of an industrial working class voicing its own demands.

24 ibid.

Stalin resurrected nationalism while flavouring it with twisted proletarian rhetoric. He encapsulated this apparent contradiction in his slogan which described the Soviet system as 'socialism in one country'. (Stalin's nationalism has matured enough for today's Bolsheviks to be able to sit and vote comfortably with the extreme nationalists and fascists of the Russian parliament).

Appropriating the safely crushed demands of the brief proletarian revolution of 1917, Stalinism purported to be leading a dominant (though as-yet non-existent) industrial working class, one portrayed as heroically non-revolutionary (self-sacrificing) and hence one which would remain state property until it finally came into existence. At this point it would be deemed obedient enough to be packaged and sold on the world market.

Various forms of Stalinism were imposed on the mainly rural areas of the twentieth-century world by the impetus of Western capitalism but not by Western capitalists themselves. Stalinism was an emergency response by embryonic bourgeoisies within backward peasant societies to the ongoing bourgeois revolution already established elsewhere.

> This underdeveloped type of ruling class was likewise a reflection of economic underdevelopment, and it had no agenda beyond correcting this backwardness in particular parts of the world. The hierarchical, statist framework of this cheap remake of the capitalist ruling class was supplied by the party of the workers organised on the bourgeois model.[25]

Far from having collapsed (as anything other than a false opposition to capitalism)[26] Stalinism emerged victorious in the 1990s. It had fulfilled its historic mission to speedily industrialise the world's remaining feudal areas through the dissolution of the world's peas-

25 *The Society of the Spectacle.*

antry while crushing and then appropriating the slogans of early
proletarian revolution:

> Stalin in fact succeeded beyond the wildest dreams of any tsarist police
> chief in destroying the Russian revolutionary movement.[27]

When in 1922 the Communist Party of the Soviet Union (as the
Bolsheviks arrogantly renamed themselves) announced that it was
leading the industrial workers to victory, it was tauntingly congrat-
ulated at its congress, 'on being the vanguard of a non-existent class
[in Russia]'.[28] Eighty percent of the Russian population were at
that time peasants. And by 1940, in this the world's first 'proletarian state', more than half the population were still peasants.

The twisted 'post-proletarian' bourgeois revolution of Stalinism
from the 1930s to the 1980s was only possible because the real proletariat was yet to come into existence there as a dominant and
potentially revolutionary class. That situation is now arising.

All power stolen from the workers' councils

The Bolsheviks' intensification of the factory system (based on
Henry Ford's Taylorism) represented its true, revolutionary introduction rather than its initial, artificial importation into a back-

26 As the workers' movement noted in the late 1960s when the Stalinist system was
   first unravelling, 'this crumbling of the worldwide alliance founded on bureaucratic
   mystification is in the last analysis the most unfavourable portent for the future
   development of capitalist society. For the bourgeoisie is now in danger of losing an
   adversary that has objectively supported it by investing all opposition to its order
   with a purely illusory unity.' (*The Society of the Spectacle.*)
27 Geoffrey Hosking, *A History of The Soviet Union, 1917–1991*, 1990.
28 ibid.

ward society by aristocrats. This intensification was proclaimed in the name of the workers by the Leninist slogan 'all power to the workers councils' because the Bolsheviks' first conquest was over the premature birth of the revolutionary working class which had succeeded in seizing Russia's first smattering of factories.

The Bolsheviks found the workers' revolution directed not at them, the future bosses, but at the temporary pseudo-bourgeoisie, the aristocrat factory owners who had come into existence under late feudalism. It became possible for embryonic Stalinism to seize the workers' revolution along with the aristocrats' factories. The Bolsheviks therefore seized this primitive workers' revolution and used it to spread an intense, hierarchical factory system in the workers' own name.

In the 1920s Lenin and Trotsky invited to Moscow American and German industrialists to assist them in imposing full-scale capitalist production. So the young millionaire, Armand Hammer, spoke for his class when he praised the Bolsheviks' strong government. This had consolidated its negotiating position in the eyes of the industrialists when it had crushed the workers at Kronstadt.

However, he voiced concern over the continuing revolutionary outlook of Russia's workers and the uncertainty this generated in business dealings with the new state. The Bolsheviks then outlined the novel qualities of their hierarchical revolution at a stroke when they assured him that theirs was officially a 'workers' government' and the trades unions could now be expected to corral the Russian workforce on their behalf. Fear of unemployment in the cities was expected to quell urban resistance to the new, intense production methods and Trotsky pledged in writing that whatever the trades unions could not control by themselves his security forces would ruthlessly smash.[29]

29 *Hammer: Witness to History.*

The workers' early revolutionary seizure of their factories was made hierarchical and reinterpreted as a revolutionary love of intense factory labour! Therefore the expedient Bolshevik slogan 'all power to the workers' councils', employed to appropriate the genius of proletarian revolution as it emerged in order to harness its innovations to the needs of dynamic capitalism, was later adjusted by Stalinists when this appropriation was complete to become the hierarchical edict, 'socialism means working hard'.

From this point onwards Stalinism represented the period of emergency during which the revolutionary seizure of the small urban working class was eclipsed by a far greater project. Stalinism was the period during which peasants were taught to work hard in modern factories.

The bemusing exhortations of Stalinist leaders as they heaped praise on their 'glorious proletariats' when, in reality, these 'proletariats' were still masses of peasants, can be seen as the 'wishing into existence' process carried out by revolutionary bourgeoisies. At the moment of their triumph in creating an industrial working class from peasantry in 1990 (and thereby completing the establishment of the factory system), the dedication of Stalinist states to the works of Karl Marx dropped swiftly away.

Earlier capitalist states had similarly abandoned the equally revolutionary works of Voltaire, Paine and Smith as talismanic guides as soon as they had succeeded in introducing an inescapable factory system in western Europe. Before this, and in an identical fashion, feudal kings had been swept away by their traders as soon as profitable trade routes had been established.

A trade route to a new working class

No sooner had new continents been discovered by explorers in the Middle Ages than European kings and queens proclaimed royal monopolies over the as-yet non-existent trade routes. Monarchs then invited adventurers to tender for the right to open up these trade routes on their behalf and turn them into reality.

In a similar fashion the Russian Bolsheviks declared themselves to be the revolutionary owners of a large industrial working class in Russia in the 1930s, long before one had come into existence.

They established a monopoly over the means of production and tendered to outside companies (such as Fiat, Krupp and, eventually, Pepsi) to help them construct in reality the working class they claimed to already possess in ideology. As a result, by 1991 the number of genuine peasants in Russia was economically insignificant (those who later 'returned to the land' due to Russia's economic crisis had no more reverted to being peasant farmers than have the scavengers on Latin America's rubbish tips).

This story is increasingly repeated in most other former Stalinist states. The appearance of mass unemployment in post-Stalinist societies is a key indicator of Stalinism's tremendous success. Workers are no longer as able to return to the countryside and are forced to seek employment in an industrial economy.

State subsidies for industry, originally put in place due to the fear that the imposition of mass unemployment would cause a significant section of the workforce to revert to peasantry, can now be done away with.

When all self-sufficiency alternatives to industrial society have been physically eliminated, the emergency rule of Stalinism can be replaced by bourgeois parliamentary democracy.

Bourgeois parliamentary democracy

The bourgeois concept of social democracy is drawn from the practice of democracy within its spontaneously formed revolutionary organisation, the joint stock limited company (a company issuing shares to investors). Therefore this is the democracy of the shareholder; the owner of the majority of shares controls the boardroom and decides the future of the company, and the souls of its workers.

As bourgeois society is the society of bourgeois investment writ large, it is no coincidence that the parliamentary democratic system mimics the majority voting principle of the boardroom. The majority factions and parties are sponsored by the most powerful shareholders and opposition parties issue manifestoes similar in style to the written overtures made by companies launching hostile takeover bids to their target's shareholders.

The democratic interests of the 'middle ground' in politics extend only as far as a concern for the minority shareholders. In this way the middle classes are always portrayed in bourgeois politics as making up the numerical bulk of the population. Official calculations of middle-class status are always archaic, cultural and vague in order to disguise the fact that the middle classes have rarely in history represented more than twenty per cent of any country's population and are today a mere tenth (literally a tithe on humanity).

Just as the bourgeoisie do not tolerate for long a democracy in which their workers have as much say as their shareholders in the running of their businesses, so bourgeois democracies are prevented or suspended during critical periods of economic growth when we first emerge as an immense social force.

Bourgeois governments, though ushering themselves in with promises of open democracy, could never hope to assemble a democratic mandate for the rapid industrialisation they are set up to introduce by the wealthy. To achieve this peasants would eventually have to vote for their own dispossession and the new class of urban workers thus created would then have to vote for slave wages. Consequently the most prolific stages of industrialisation in

Western nations during the nineteenth century were all overseen by profoundly undemocratic bourgeois governments: examples include England before the Reform Bill, France under Louis Napoleon, Germany under Bismarck, and even America, where the bourgeoisie pioneered the technique of transferring democracy to their bankers during the emergency period of the civil war.

With the advent of the twentieth century the pressing need for rapid industrialisation in the remaining feudal areas meant that emergent bourgeoisies dispensed with any semblance of democracy in their revolution.

The rich were furious that by the 1920s rural economic backwardness was robbing them of potential profits on one hand while their factories were falling to a wave of revolutionary uprisings and occupations on the other. Workers in Northern Italy had almost succeeded in abolishing capitalism there until the bourgeoisie used their parliament to vote democracy out of existence in favour of Fascism. The persistence of too large a peasant population in an industrial Germany, also on the brink of working-class revolution, caused a temporary democracy there to be repealed by an anxious bourgeoisie from 1931 onwards.

Only when peasants have been driven off the land and the factory system and labour discipline (industrial alienation) have been properly established will bourgeois governments risk bestowing universal suffrage on working people. Only when factory managers report that the revolutionary movement of the workers (our immediate demand for democratic control of our lives at work) has been broken will the bourgeoisie begin to allow us to vote in parliamentary elections.

Because bourgeois political parties only emerge during or after the defeat of direct worker democracy, and are therefore based on hierarchical structures, there is no danger that they will dispossess the rich on election no matter what manifesto pledges they have issued. The bourgeoisie know that, as we are beaten, our options are limited. We will accept the alienated range of choices at the ballot box that we have already been forced to accept at work, the choice between more or less shopping with our wages (credit or austerity), whichever is deemed best for the good of the (bourgeois) nation.

It is this encouragement under bourgeois democracy to subsume our real needs, problems and desires within the mythical needs and suffering of 'the nation' (which are in reality the needs and suffering of the monopoly rich against us) that characterises modern bourgeois politics and finds its first mass expression in Nazism.

Nazi Revolution: Germany 1933

The Hitlerian dictatorship which replaced the Weimar republic in Germany can be viewed as the bourgeois revolution against vestigial feudalism perfected and the emergence of the first prototype bourgeois democratic party of the industrial era which could be safely offered by the rich to an almost full electorate.

Until the 1920s parliamentary suffrage in so-called democracies was generally still restricted to landlords (the property qualification). The ruling class feared that the workers (male and female), if given the vote, would elect governments that would tax them out of existence (i.e. extend into parliament the revolution they had already launched in their workplaces).

The creation of National Socialist democracy, a dictatorship designed to resemble democracy while restricting it exclusively to a controllable parliament by crushing workplace democracy, indicated that it was becoming safe to allow the share-register finally to supplant the rent-roll as the basis of modern society.

The Nazi Party was manoeuvred into power on a wave of advertising by monopoly capitalists (Krupp, Thyssen and, in part, Ford) who erected the heroic, billboard myth of a suffering nation before an electorate who were not in reality required to elect it (because these firms had already sponsored the middle-class unemployed to 'vote with their knuckle-dusters' for it on the streets).

The Nazis rallied the German bourgeoisie behind the war manifesto of their arms-manufacturer backers, a manifesto pledged to reopen forcefully the underdeveloped markets of the East and reclaim the bad debts that nations there had reneged on.

Domestically the Nazi Party established all the slogans of today's bourgeois democracy, the vow to create a 'classless society' (while protecting private property), and the need to serve *Mittelstandsideologie* (middle-class ideology), the interests of the middle-class 'majority' who were less than twenty per cent of the population and whose numbers were rapidly and permanently being diminished by capitalism.

Once in power the Nazis 'passed laws which contributed more to the economic annihilation of their former voters than any other regime had dared before'.[30]

Having declared that they would champion the small businessman and the small peasant farmer (who voted and fought for them) the Nazis unleashed the cartelisation processes of big business, the department stores, the agricultural industry and urban-property companies which swept their voters into history.

Having proclaimed a middle-class revolution they in fact put the entire country at the disposal of their backers – the monopoly capitalists – and launched immense industrialisation, with the military employed by the state to assist the largest capitalist combines in their rush for growth and their need for new infrastructure.

The Nazis honoured the bourgeoisie's Hegelian principles of planning, modernisation, state power and national progress in their

30 *The Economy and Class Structure of German Fascism.*

rhetoric and redefined social revolution as bourgeois violence against the workers; a 'revolution from above' that ruthlessly crushed fifty per cent of the population by holding industrial wages at the level of 1932 throughout the regime before finally hurling them into prolicidal (and suicidal) warfare.

As a perfect bourgeois revolution, Nazism was non-asset-seizing (capitalist property was safe). The state carried out instead a pseudo-social revolution. It sanctioned the legalistic seizure of 'Jewish property' as an alienated parody of the spontaneous revolutionary seizure of large-scale private property by workers during proletarian revolutions.

'The Jews' were an invented class, fabricated around an ethnic group but in reality extended to include any obstacle to unfettered monopoly capitalism from trades unionists to those physically unable to earn profits for big business, the disabled. They were offered as a target to the public by the bourgeoisie as an alienated substitute for the rich themselves.

The invented struggle of the suffering nation dragged down by weakness and conspiracy was the state-sanctioned replacement for class anger at the working class being dragged down by alienation.

The manufactured icon of the Nazi Revolution, Adolf Hitler, was sponsored by bourgeois industrialists to be their revolutionary spokesman for planning and monopoly. His name was calculated to thrill the middle classes with its similarity to that of their great hero up until then, the man who had directed the experimental fascism of Bonapartism half a century before, Adolphe Thiers.

Thiers' programme to 'finish socialism forever' (the erotic dream of all bourgeois superstars), was subsumed to a far greater level within Hitler's. Thiers had lead the bourgeois revolution in France against the workers and crushed all proletarian revolutions there from 1848 up to the Paris Commune. He had praised the army he was forced to govern with as the 'representatives of democracy'.

When he came to power, Hitler was able to enlist a great many more of the electorate to bolster his claims of army democracy because the logic of nationalism had progressed so handsomely in the intervening decades (in effect, with Hitler the ruling classes of the West explored how to repackage the career of Thiers as a swastika-emblazoned titan before finally understanding how to mass-produce the format of 'saviour of the suffering nation' for democratic consumption as 'Thatcherists' once the bourgeois nation was finally fully established in the 1990s).

As the perfected bourgeois revolution is nationalist so, within it, the hierarchy-abolishing class struggle of the workers reappears, but in the alienated and hierarchical form of a 'racial struggle'. This has made Hitler – in preference to Lenin – a nationalist role model for revolutionary army officers in developing countries richer in assets than in peasantry, especially where departing colonialism has left a legacy of ethnic stratification.

As a bourgeois revolution, the Nazi revolution was primarily industrialising and quickly dissolved the remaining peasantry (in their own name!) under the Farm Inheritance Act. This Act, allegedly designed to protect feudal Germany from capitalism, in reality forced peasant families to sell out their farms to large-scale agricultural cartels. This 'cartelisation' thus produced a similar effect to the state collectivisation of farms in the Soviet Union under Stalin.

> In direct opposition to the ideological principle of giving preference to the farmers and peasants during the Third Reich, 700,000 farm labourers were moved into the cities to work in industry.[31]

The Nazi revolution in Germany pioneered methods of servicing

---

31 Otto-Ernst Schüddekopf, *Revolutions of Our Time: Fascism, 1973.*

the new needs of large-scale capitalism. The Farm Inheritance Act was an early appearance of state planning legislation. Planning systems were to become ubiquitous to industrial nations after World War Two. Their function is the planning of towns through the rationalisation of the countryside – i.e. the abolition of a rural economy and the urbanisation of the countryside.

The function of emergency bourgeois dictatorships such as Nazism or Stalinism is therefore to break the revolution of the workers and transcend the peasant class by forcing it into the factory system, based at first in large cities.

The peasantry is transcended into a proletariat and this new proletariat is then crushed through terror and through competition with the influx of further cheap and desperate new workers still arriving from the land.

THE HAMSTER WHEEL

The early factory system

When first confronted by the factory system in the eighteenth and nineteenth centuries, workers openly attacked it, burning down factories and destroying machinery. They did this in the legalistic belief that they were enforcing feudal laws against the manufacture of poor-quality, non-guild-certified goods (laws that capitalism first 'repealed' through its production methods before establishing bourgeois governments to repeal them in statute).

This then became the period of bloody murder for peasants and early industrial workers as the owners of the factory system set out to defend their investments. Army units roamed the countryside to protect industrial equipment, spreading terror outside the factories while managers spread terror within them. This was the 'block-house' era of the factory. Life outside the factory system was crim-inalised, life within it was regimented and oppressive.

All peasants and early industrial workers were suspected of sab-otage. The purge of the Luddites in the nineteenth century reap-peared in its industrialised form as full-blown extermination in the twentieth-century. During this period life outside the factory was not merely criminalised but made into the capital offence of war against civilians (appearing as the state collectivisation of farms, world war, etc.).

Once the production techniques of industrial capitalism had been established (and the resultant super production had begun to plunge those outside the factories trying to compete with them into penury) the terror against workers could be eased. It was no longer necessary to drive workers into the factories as enclosure increasingly divorced them from an alternative life on the land.

Peasants and artisans were also unable to support themselves outside the system by selling handicrafts as markets were now swamped with cheaply produced industrial goods (such as textiles) against which they could not hope to compete. Even workers with access to their own small-holdings could not support themselves outside the factory.

At this point the workers accepted the logic of capitalism, political economy, and rushed to form 'combinations'. They attempted, by banding together, to drive up the cost of the only market product left for them to sell, their own labour.

Social progress as a by-product of the factory system

Because the bourgeoisie are revolutionary, their practice, capitalism, is a progressive social force. So it is important to note that an unanticipated by-product of the early factory system (from the capitalists' point of view) was the growing liberation of the workers, starting with the liberation of women which its spread brought about (and continues to bring about).

Despite the harsh discipline imposed by early factory owners, young women were nevertheless able to free themselves from the harsher patriarchal constraints of the rural village by moving to the manufacturing districts and seeking employment in the factories.

Although women represented cheap labour for the bourgeoisie, for themselves their wages were their first opportunity to obtain a semi-independent life. Young women workers could afford (or were provided with) accommodation near to work and could thus escape the rural destiny of an arranged marriage, where the domestic drudgery of youth (assisting their mothers) lead, in an unbroken line, directly to the domestic drudgery of serving a husband (motherhood).

Here, if only enjoyed as a brief hiatus, commenced the freedom and independence of youth in the cities which began to destroy the patriarchal oppression of feudalism – in the process eroding the grip of that feudal overlord of all women, organised religion.

This semi-independence for women led to semi-independence for all workers and to the beginnings of a new type of society. As observers have noted:

> … the claim that the Industrial Revolution raised the status of women would seem to have little meaning when set beside the record of excessive hours of labour, cramped housing, excessive child-bearing and terrifying rates of child mortality. On the other hand, the abundant opportunities for female employment [in the factory system] gave women the status of independent wage-earners.[32]

As the factory system spread, so did the possibility of women's liberation (and therefore human liberation). Women migrated from the villages and in the cities the numbers of prostitutes declined as demand for factory workers increased.[33] But the owners of the factory system did not welcome this unintended side-effect of their profit system. The bourgeoisie continued to regard wives and

32 *The Making of the English Working Class.*
33 Ibid.

daughters as private property, and so an incredible situation arose where wealthy women experienced less freedom than peasant girls in the early stages of the factory system.

The bourgeoisie responded to this by raising patriarchy (the control of the workforce) up to a political level (the subsumption of patriarchy under national legislation).

The war against 'public immorality' (rights to abortion, divorce, sexual freedom, homosexuality, etc.) saw (and is still seeing) the capitalist class attempting to place its genii back into the bottle. In trying it has become enmeshed in a dialectic between its need to 'liberate' urban workers from their rural families (their former owners) and its need for them to behave as disciplined labour.

What is vital to note is that the wildest theories about the creation of a 'new type of humanity' and the prospect of sexual equality, publicly funded abortion, the end of the family unit, etc., held out by feminists and anarchists in the late 1700s has, as a result of the above effect, been realised in unremarkable fashion through the daily reality of life under the factory system in the twentieth century; but without any of the accompanying hope that this liberation would be linked to social freedom.

As noted by the earliest theorists of the working class, the factory system makes possible the liberation of its workforce but this possibility can only be truly realised if that workforce unites and seizes hold of the means of production.

Strikes

Whatever the social benefits of the factory town are in comparison to the peasant village for women, as soon as factory work becomes established the bourgeoisie begin to drive down wages for all workers. The first weapon developed by workers to raise the price of labour in defiance of this move was the strike.

The invention of the strike by early industrial workers was a sign of their genius. It demonstrated their incredible ability to adapt swiftly to any social terrain constructed against them by the bourgeoisie and combat them on it. The strike was the feudal peasant revolt refashioned by industrial workers into a sophisticated, precision tool for class struggle.

Peasants were unable to defend themselves by going on strike, withholding their labour or occupying their fields. Peasants could threaten to withhold their feudal dues (the extra, unpaid labour due their landlord which evolved under capitalism into surplus labour) but as they were geographically isolated their landlord's reaction was to treat this as an almost military act of defiance. The only means by which peasants could 'go on strike' was through arming themselves and mounting an insurrection. All the accompanying dangers of armed insurgency followed. To ensure the legality of their rising, peasants frequently allied their revolts to the cause of a noble 'pretender' to the throne or appealed to their landlord or king to ignore 'bad counsel' and rule with their help.

This need to legalise individual peasant revolts doomed them to failure. Repeatedly peasants were routed and crushed as aristocratic order was reaffirmed. This was until the peasants allied themselves not to a single pretender, but to the cause of an entire class of pretenders arising out of their own ranks, the bourgeoisie.

Revolts eventually became so general and total that a new level of consciousness emerged – peasants realised that they could only legalise their uprisings by abolishing the aristocracy altogether and establishing democracy (to rule by themselves without the king's help). At this point peasants carried out revolutions, though in doing so they transferred their attachment from the cause of a royal pretender to the broader canvas of the aspirations of an emerging bourgeoisie.

Just as peasants knew of no greater nightmare than that experi-

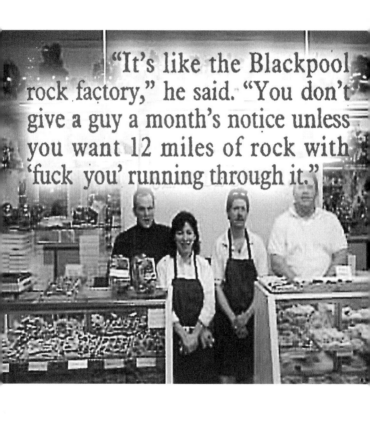

"It's like the Blackpool rock factory," he said. "You don't give a guy a month's notice unless you want 12 miles of rock with 'fuck you' running through it."

enced in the aftermath of an unsuccessful uprising (when they were usually slaughtered on the battlefield), so later industrial workers learned that they could expect no greater agony than that undergone during the industrialised version of the peasant revolt, the strike, in their unequal struggle with the bourgeois class in power, the capitalists.

During these crises the capitalist class relished its newly acquired ability to starve workers back to work. But the strike, like the revolt for the peasants, began to awaken in the workers an understanding of the gigantic task in front of them. Workers began to understand that, unlike peasants, they were united by the factory system. Even where they were geographically separated they were linked together through the reciprocal needs of production. When they stopped work, backlogs appeared as the lack of materials required by other parts of the system forced other workers and bosses to experience the effects of their strike. Workers began to see that while single strikes – and even a whole series of strikes – could eventually be broken, it would be theoretically possible to spread a 'general strike' across all sectors of the economy and in all areas of the world at once.

As the factory system integrated more and more of the world's economy, the use of the general strike as a weapon became a stronger possibility in the minds of workers. They saw that it would be a situation which capitalists would be incapable of containing. It was not the price of labour which workers needed to raise but the entire society of capitalist labour itself which they needed to overturn.

With this historic insight workers recognised themselves as being, at least potentially, a class. Becoming their own cause and their own 'pretenders to the throne', they announced their programme, the first slogan of which was: 'workers of the world unite, we have nothing to lose but our chains' (proclaimed in 1847).

Here then is the origin of workers' demands which, unlike those for higher wages or shorter working hours, can never be met, even briefly, by the bourgeois class (without it abolishing itself). But the capitalists recognised the danger of the strike as well.

In sitting out strikes they lost money and so gave advantage to their rivals. In addition, the concept of solidarity which was awoken in their workers (and the dawning of the general strike theory) posed a very serious threat to all other bosses as by design its message was to their workers too.

Pressure mounted among the bourgeoisie for strikes to be crushed and, where this failed, for a system of settlements to be established in order to contain workers' demands and prevent strikes from spreading. The strike began to be a regular feature of industrial life (though not necessarily a permanent one).

The spontaneous committees of the workers, in attempting to organise food and community survival during strikes, became the first means by which workers realised that they could organise the whole of society for themselves. These later hardened into representatives who sought to negotiate on their behalf with the bosses. These 'trades unions' therefore ossified class consciousness at the moment of its first emergence, retaining the consciousness of a working class still divided among the competing trades of early capitalism.

In their rhetoric the trades unions endlessly perpetuated the moment at which feudal workers realised that under industrial conditions they could form a single class but without capturing the revolutionary conclusions then drawn by this new class. At a political level trades unions were, and still are, simple, theatrical performances put on to re-enact this moment while never evolving beyond it. The most obvious indication of this is the very concept of 'trades unions' as this term implies a continuing belief in the late feudal separation of labour into guilds of skilled tradesmen.

Trades unions, unlike revolutionary workers' councils, are hopelessly unable to deal with the capitalist invention of mass unemployment as the feudal, urban unemployed were despised by guild workers (who 'closed' their workshops against them).

The feudal logic of trades unions forces them to regard the mass unemployed (created by capitalism as an essential part of its inert proletariat) as some monstrous class of sturdy beggars, vagabonds and jugglers whom they can pity but are unable to assist, and indeed must resist.

The unemployed cannot be understood by the trades union movement as anything other than a threat to employed workers' wages. Unemployment is the trades unions' greatest horror because it harks back to the conditions of the feudal guild wherein the ability to sack an apprentice, once they were honoured enough to be accepted by a master, was quite weak.

But unemployment is merely the extended logic of the misery of alienated labour.

Trades unions

Despite one hundred and fifty years of widespread trades union activity the gulf between wealth and poverty in the most advanced economic areas of the world is now wider than it was a century ago. The unavoidable conclusion is that trades unions are not the revolutionary form of proletarian resistance to the factory system, nor of the proletariat realising our class status. Yet, because the severe problems we experience daily at work obscure from us our historic fundamental problem of capitalism itself, we continue to seek the protection of trades unions.

The failure of trades unions to develop revolutionary consciousness arises from the fact that they are hierarchies whose everyday function is not social but economic:

the trade unions aim at nothing less than to prevent the reduction of wages below the level that is traditionally maintained in the various branches of industry. That is to say, they wish to prevent the price of labour-power from falling below its value … For this reason the unions never allow their members to work for less than the minimum [wage]. They are insurance societies formed by the workers themselves.[34]

But as capitalist society wields its increasingly awesome power to extract relative surplus value on a global scale, the task of policing a minimum wage for workers on a piecemeal sector by sector basis is rapidly marginalised. Gradually the political activity of trades unions starts to become a hindrance and then a threat to us. The trades unions' economic goal of policing the commodity price of collected labour-power which it negotiates to sell to the employers on our behalf begins to manifest itself politically as the policing of the labour force to preserve the value of the commodity it is selling.

Trades unions thus start to isolate grievances which might act as a catalyst to organised resistance to the factory system itself (the destruction of the employers) and to deal with these grievances at an individualised level.

They further remove grievances from our consciousness by 'dealing with them on our behalf', or otherwise mediating through the employers' procedures for isolating them.

The political purpose of trades unions starts to resemble a firefighting exercise to prevent organised resistance (wildcat strikes and occupation movements) from forming and to channel any which do emerge towards ultimately impotent forms of protest.

Because trades unions restrict themselves to protecting their members, and then in purely economic terms (a task always out-

34 Karl Marx, *Capital*, 1867.

paced by the vast expansion of the world economy), they become incorporated into capitalism's management system. However, they are not a defence mechanism developed by the capitalist system itself as most capitalists remain implacably hostile to their existence. Without doubt most employers regard mass unemployment as the most effective means of isolating worker grievances and of setting a fair price for labour.

They only take advantage of the trades unions' natural inclination to control their workforces once tight labour markets have arisen (as in periods of skills shortage) or when proletarian unrest is affecting other areas of society. This institutional role played by trades unions in advanced areas appears remarkably similar to that played by Stalinism in backward ones, to promote a (bourgeois) revolutionary dedication to the factory system in those parts of that system that produce the highest levels of worker disillusionment.

The Marxist rhetoric of the semi-skilled workers' trades union movement (in the West) up until the 1980s mimicked exactly that of the industrialising Stalinist states in the East.

Trades union leaders, like Stalinists, are a potential class of emergency bourgeoisie, although as they operate under an already victorious bourgeoisie most are destined to perish continuously at the larval stage, never attaining state power above gaining a sinecure in company management or becoming a government bureaucrat.[35]

---

35 But as the career path of Cyril Ramaphosa has demonstrated, a period of social upheaval can enable an astute trades union leader to unite with management as a new boss. Once the 'militant' leader of South Africa's miners' union, Ramaphosa used the collapse of apartheid to elevate himself to the board of the Anglo-American mining company he was supposed to have been protecting his members against. He became a multi-millionaire.

Like Stalinists though they exhort us to fight for 'full employment' under a planned economy (that is to fight for universal alienated factory labour under themselves as the emergency bourgeoisie in power) instead of demanding the abolition of work altogether.

As they seek the highest price for the commodity they aim to sell to employers, trades union leaders dream of a workforce which has fallen in love with hard work. After all, this would be the highest quality their commodity could achieve and therefore the easiest to sell. Beyond this they dream of a society in which they replace, or merge with the employers altogether in order to ensure that their members become a high-quality, expensive commodity. In other words they dream of becoming guild-masters within a capitalist society – syndicalism.

It is the mass rejection of work by workers in the most monotonous and primitive areas of the factory system which therefore poses the greatest threat to both militant trades unions and factory bosses as it implies the abolition of them both.

Syndicalism

Unlike their political goal of full employment, the highest form of radicalism that a trades union is capable of theorising (though never of putting into effect) is that of syndicalism. Syndicalism, or workers' control, is the pure dream of the trades union movement divorced from its actual practice in modern society.

Syndicalism does exist, but only among workers from the social elite: academics, surgeons, barristers, senior police officers and top civil servants. For much of the twentieth century these 'trades' enjoyed self-regulating status with little management constraint, firstly because such independence poses little threat to the capitalist state, and secondly because capitalism has yet to extend proletarianisation into these areas.

The trades union movement's desire to extend syndicalism to all workers can never be realised. This is because it is nothing more than the stunted yearning of the movement to return their workers to the feudal protection of the medieval guild while reforming it – in other words, to dream of overthrowing all guild masters. But because guild-masters are figures that history has long since replaced with global capitalists, trades unions yearn to resurrect them in monstrous form; re-embodied as the governing committees of a federated trades union movement taking over capitalism from capitalists and turning it into a global guild workshop.

In any case it is no revolutionary position to advocate the ownership by workers of their specific trades and factories (the Balkanisation of the workplaces!). In illustration of this, the syndicalism of senior medical consultants has not caused them to adopt a radical approach to medical practice. Though free to explore their profession these consultants fail daily to diagnose the most easily identifiable source of most ill-health, capitalist society, let alone prescribe an effective treatment for it.

But this insight is of course gained immediately by revolutionary medical students when they join workers councils and seize their medical faculties, throwing them open for public discussion, as occurred during the 1968 French revolution.[36]

While syndicalism aims to preserve the privileges of a worker elite (demarcated into 'trades'), only the revolutionary seizure of all society by the entire proletariat together through the formation of workers' councils can effectively begin the abolition of class society. This is a conclusion that we, the workers, have arrived at early on in our struggle.

The point at which workers attempted general or social syndi-

---

36 See for instance the leaflet 'Medicine and Repression' put out by the French National Young Doctor's Centre in 1968.

calism in Britain – the placing of all industry and the country under the control of a federated trades union movement as a method of peacefully overthrowing capitalism (the Yugoslavia of the workplaces!) – came in 1834 with the short-lived project of the 'Grand National Consolidated Trades Union'. And an attempt at social syndicalism has been a stage passed through by most labour movements in their struggles.

But this faith in social syndicalism as a solution to early industrial capitalism is a transitory stage only. It is rapidly eclipsed in the hearts of the workers who have been fighting to establish it as soon as they realise the tremendous possibilities and global social transformations opened up by bourgeois society in and outside of the workplace.

Immediately they understand how pedestrian the aim of merely managing industry and trade through a hierarchical trades union organisation has become. Forcing the workers to aim higher are the bourgeoisie themselves, who are ruthless in defeating syndicalist schemes aimed at peacefully removing their ownership of the workforce. Social syndicalism is as forcefully smashed by the bourgeoisie as are all half-measures raised against its revolution.

So it is the revolutionary power of workers' councils, first tentatively exemplified by the Paris Commune, which aims at nothing less than the total seizure of all of society so that human creative evolution can become the conscious choice and project of a united human race. Workers' councils become the recognised vehicles for proletarian revolution rather than reform.

Their appearance reveals to all classes that revolutionary consciousness can directly embody power. At this point the bourgeois-dissolving ambition to abolish work makes its appearance.

The goal of the revolutionary workers movement becomes the desire not to seize hold of the mere organisation of labour but consciously to seize the entire global planning system of world capitalism and unleash the pent-up historical collective mission of the human race which capitalism has stunted at the primitive and alienated level of economics.

By contrast social syndicalism, as a phase already passed over, can only ever offer the perpetuation of work run more efficiently and humanely by labour organisations instead of by capitalists. However, few if any of today's global trades unions aim even as high as the superseded dream of social syndicalism.

Today's trades union movement dreams of a limited syndicalism which is only the radical desire of medieval apprentices to do away with their guild masters unnaturally preserved into modern times. This necrophilic nostalgia (underlined by repeated calls for the return of apprenticeship schemes) causes the trades union movement to cling to demands from antiquity as its highest contemporary expression. It has nothing progressive to offer.

If it were to face for one moment the reality of life for its members under modern capitalism, the trades union movement would transform itself immediately into a self-abolishing revolutionary movement (thence advocating 'anarcho-syndicalism' or revolutionary workers' control) or else simply dissolve itself into such a movement.

Socialism

Even if the trades union movement, unlike the working class, is unwilling to advocate the revolutionary overthrow of capitalist society, bizarrely this aspiration has been voiced by some early industrial capitalists themselves. Alongside the brutality and oppression of the primitive factory system (which is based on conditions as near as possible to those of slavery) exists the advanced factory system which employs the latest technologies and working practices. Working conditions in this sector have always had to be better than those in the more backward parts of the system in order to attract and retain a skilled workforce. It is in this advanced sector that trades unions often boast that they have won concessions which in reality have been granted in advance by the owners.

So awestruck have some capitalists been when they have fully comprehended the power of advanced industrialism and the latent potential of the enormous workforces assembled to operate it that a handful have fleetingly glimpsed the Utopian potential of modern society which lies underneath their system. But any conscious recognition of this they normally shield both from themselves and their workers.

These bosses have realised that the impact of their factories is socially revolutionary. But because they are bosses and already possess a social dictatorship at work they extinguish this flicker of revolutionary consciousness and don instead the arrogant mantle of social reformer.

This is not at all an altruistic position; by raising levels of education, wages and living standards in contradiction to their natural inclination to impoverish the working class these bosses increase the productivity of their factories, the quality of their commodities and are able, through having skilled and healthy workers, to introduce more sophisticated technology than their more brutal competitors. Furthermore their workers are able to save enough money to become a 'workforce of consumption' after work and thus complete the circle of exploitation through shopping.

The result has been super profits from these sunrise factories throughout the history of industrialisation. Even when they seem superficially 'well paid', in real terms workers are being impoverished due to the accelerating gulf between their wages and the new oceanic scale of their 'enlightened' bosses' wealth.

Robert Owen pioneered the humane, advanced factory in the early 1800s. His partners in the immense cotton mills he owned (which at that time represented high technology) were initially horrified at his leniency towards their workers until they saw the gigantic profit margins generated. Owen envisaged his factories changing the whole face of society and thus termed his business strategy 'socialism'.

The occasional socialist factory owner has followed Owen's early lucrative example. The German industrialist Friedrich Engels even mutinied from his class and actually joined the workers' movement before eventually returning to run his Manchester factories after 1851 (thus demonstrating that some members of the bourgeoisie could, conceivably, be absorbed by a proletarian revolution).

But although a few industrial capitalists of the nineteenth century brought over to our movement details of the ruling class's secret – that our world can become a Utopia without them – by the twentieth century modern capitalists had learnt to extract the profit-boosting aspects of humane 'socialism' while doing away with any concept of abolishing capitalism.

The manufacturer Henry Ford pioneered this high-waged 'sociological' approach which he openly admitted was designed to produce workers whose home life was forced to be so sober and thrifty that they could afford to buy his motor cars.

Socialism is the progressive face of capitalism wherever its technology is at its most advanced. It is a business strategy designed to raise our loyalty to the companies owned by the rich almost to the level of revolutionary fervour and it openly incorporates the trades union movement within it. But the project of socialism is doomed to fail for the simple reason that all advanced sectors of capitalism quickly become low-skilled, monotonous and primitive sectors within the space of a decade or so as technology advances beyond them.

In any case, no matter how socially advanced working conditions become it is the Utopia-destroying alienation of social hierarchy that makes our work dismal. No socialist trick can dispel our painful knowledge that we are wasting our lives working for the benefit of others in a prefabricated world built to accommodate their profit system instead of our happiness. And this is a world on the brink of becoming even more intensely fabricated today.

FASTER!!

The next phase of the bourgeois revolution

As former Stalinist societies integrate with the West (for both boom and bust) and the trades union movement gingerly flexes the qualified role allowed it by capitalists, the bourgeois revolution in the most advanced nations is starting on another profound transition. Capitalism is revolutionary in its aim to establish a global proletariat – at the moment this global proletariat is created the bourgeois revolution will be complete in its own terms.

The bourgeois definition of a proletarianised world is one in which both labour and leisure time are 'subsumed under capital'. This is a situation in which every waking moment of a worker's life is an uninterrupted experience either of factory labour (the regimented labour of the office, factory, retail unit or commercial hotel etc) or of intensified shopping.

To realise this vision, capitalism is embarking on a further revolutionary social transformation in the most advanced countries. This is termed the move from the 'formal to the real subsumption of leisure under capital' as it arises from the real subsumption of labour under capital from the nineteenth century onwards.

Early capitalism: the formal subsumption of labour under capital

When the workers' movement began to analyse its situation in the mid-nineteenth century it rapidly identified the central movement of industrial capitalism at that time, a movement so profound it was creating an entirely new form of society, capitalist society. This was theorised by the worker' movement as it studied its position under the Industrial Revolution and expressed in political economic terms in Marx's *Capital*, the key theoretical text, with the somewhat clumsy expression: 'the movement from the formal to the real subsumption of labour under capital'.

Subsumption theory

Exploitation, unpaid labour performed for profit, has been subsumed within an industrial system. The movement identified occurs in two distinct phases. Firstly feudal craft labour is increasingly sucked beneath (subsumed by) the logic of early mercantile capitalism. Then a critical moment is reached when it can no longer expand further under the old system of organisation and so suddenly tips over into the whirlwind of revolutionary industrial factory organisation.

This 'tipping over' occurred in the nineteenth century in the advanced economic areas with the introduction of steam-driven machinery. A proper understanding of this movement reveals the structure of its vast acceleration in our own times.

The first stage of the movement, (first witnessed from the late middle ages up until the late eighteenth century) is termed by political economy the 'formal subsumption of labour under capital' because it is the subsumption of labour in a primitive manner and corresponds to processes of the early, pre-industrial capitalist era.

Under formal subsumption the medieval workshop is seized

upon by early capitalism. It is then enlarged, multiplied and extended and the quality of its craftsmanship is debased. Essentially it retains the same form as the guilded craft workshop of feudalism but now monstrously stretched, distorted and degraded on an ever-increasing scale.

The former craftsmen of the feudal production system, few in number and jealous of their hard-earned skills, find that their numbers are massively multiplied and the length of their working days brutally extended under early capitalist control. Their stern but attentive and knowledgeable guild-masters are also multiplied by early capitalism into a plethora of less-skilled overseers and taskmasters.

In raising its legion of petty time-keepers from the larval stage of the guild-master, capitalism casts aside his role as a traditional guarantor of craft quality and accentuates their role as strict discipliners of labour time. But this mammoth 'sweating down' of craft workers into 'hands' and the bastardisation of guild-masters into overseers only manages to lay the ground conditions for a proper capitalist society.

Industrial capitalism: the real subsumption of labour under capital

The logic of capitalist accumulation demands that it breaks through any apparently unbreachable barriers.

Even though they might work themselves to death, no-one can work longer than 24 hours in a day, nor can a factory building be extended across whole counties or an overseer watch every worker for every minute to ensure maximum productivity.

To overcome these obstacles capitalism embarks on a qualitative transition which in turn alters the entire fabric of society in advanced economic areas.

Large-scale power-driven machinery is invented to replace the former process of simply multiplying workshop benches and extending factories. Now the individual tools of the workers, instead of being endlessly multiplied, suddenly spring out of their hands and rear up into monstrous sizes before them. Scissors, which could only cut cloth before, now become massive shears, fifty feet high and able to slice through cold steel. Hand-held hammers mushroom up into steel-pounding Titans which nevertheless remain precision tools.

With these new machines an industrial worker (a 'really subsumed' labourer) can perform in each hour the equivalent of a week's continuous work by a hundred former craftsmen ('formally subsumed' labourers).

Furthermore, these machines are fuel-driven. Factory managers need no longer watch every worker. Now they need only set the speed of the new machines to dictate the pace of the working day. Heavy industrial equipment therefore becomes the workers' constantly vigilant mechanical overseer, determining the predictable and endlessly repeated amount of time needed to produce a single item, regulating quality (or lack of it) and homogenising the form it will have to take.

This process finally removes forever any creative element that the workers may previously have added to their products. (We can only now recover that creative input into our products by seizing the entire productive system world-wide.)

The result is the super-production of cheap and basically assembled goods by industrial workers engaged in mindless work at one end of the social pole, and mass unemployment at the other.

This introduction of large-scale power tools and the consequent revolutionisation of the workplace (and of society, now formed around huge industrial cities as a result) have been termed in the critique of political economy carried out by the workers' movement of the nineteenth century, the 'real subsumption of labour under capital'.

The surplus labour of each worker (our unpaid exploitation), amplified by the actions of huge machinery, produces industrial capitalist society proper, a society now dominated by big cities centred around industrial production instead of being rurally focused around peasant agriculture.

In tandem with the introduction of large-scale machinery revolutionising craft labour into industrial work, the feudal division of labour (the dividing up by the guild-master of the different stages in the assembly of complicated goods between different workbenches in the old workshop) was also subsumed by the whirlwind of 'real' capitalist production to reappear as the mechanised production line of the total factory.

Now a factory armed with large-scale machinery and an automated assembly line could rapidly flood the globe with cheap manufactured goods. These techniques introduced into farming (as mechanised agricultural equipment, applied chemistry and the agglomeration of meadows into huge, hedgeless fields or 'vegetable factories') had the profound effect of sinking the cost of food to almost nothing. Many farmers were ruined in the early twentieth century as food prices slumped (and giant farming companies were then able to step in and buy up their farms en masse). The incredible possibility of industrial society, a world of unlimited abundance, first manifested itself in the destruction of profitable farming and the creation of virtually free food.

Of course this incredible breakthrough was presented as a economic crisis rather than an indication of the success of industrialisation at freeing humanity from want.

In order to maintain the level of food prices for the newly created cartels, some governments colluded in the mass hoarding and destruction of food stuffs. But capitalist society, as ever, discovered a more revolutionary solution to over-production. The social effects of this solution are now transforming our society as totally as in the last century.

Cybernetic capitalism: the real subsumption of leisure under capital

Today the next gigantic movement in capitalist accumulation is occurring in the developed world. Leisure, our free time after work, must increasingly be colonised in order to meet the 'realisation' demands of modern capitalism.

'Realisation' is shopping and consumption. Surplus value is extracted from us at work because we are only paid real wages for a fragment of our working day, the rest we are forced to give away. This free bonus which capitalists award themselves off our backs cannot be immediately collected because it is fused into the abundance of commodities we have made. It can only be placed into their pockets as immense profits if it can be 'realised', that is if it can be sold.

After exploiting us in the workplace the bourgeoisie must therefore desperately court us after work in order to complete the full circle of investment and cream off the surplus value stolen from us (i.e. sell the world we have just created back to us in a predictable form over which we have no creative control and at a profit).

The old city centres with their rows of shops are simply not efficient enough to match the insatiable realisation demands of super-industrialised capitalism as it over-produces wildly. They must be revolutionised which requires another total transformation of society with the abolition of the urban high street and its replacement with its gargantuan equivalent, the total leisure shopping environment. This is the movement from the formal to the real subsumption of leisure under capital.

NO SHOP-LIFTING

SHOPPING

The subsumption of the high street

Taking the United Kingdom as a model, we can chart the subsumption of the urban high street into the leisure shopping environment after the total imposition of the advanced factory system following World War 2.

The devastation of bombing established a cycle of total reconstruction of the built environment as a permanent feature of modern society. By orchestrating and facilitating this process the state planning system continued the effects of bombing into peacetime. This policy has been termed by the workers' movement 'urbanism'.

In the 1960s the state began to address the urgent realisation needs of capitalism by linking together urban areas with transport networks and supply depots, and reconstructing them, at first crudely, around the sole principle of large-scale shopping (consumer goods produced and distributed by large-scale capitalists rather than those supplied by local producers):

> an improved motorway network and rising living standards led to warehouse development on the urban fringes and town centre

redevelopment being promoted by local authorities. It is during this
period that many of the typical 1960s shopping centres were constructed
of monolithic concrete construction, open to the elements and with little
to attract shoppers into the centre other than the necessity to shop.[37]

Being so colossal, the output of the post-war factory system drove
the logic of urban planning and redevelopment. Urbanism
advanced rapidly in all ascendent economic countries, not merely
the UK. After the advent of the shopping centre (a term which
expresses as clearly as possible the fact that the centre of towns, formerly industrial, now become increasingly devoted to shopping)
evolution was swift, as explained by a property investment analyst
in the 1990s:

> The history of town centre schemes has been relatively short; they are
> principally a phenomenon of the 1960s onwards, but it has been a history
> of rapid change from the early uncovered centres of the 1960s through to
> the fully air-conditioned centres of the 1970s … most shopping centre
> developments have involved institutional funds and they provide
> numerous examples of co-operation between local authorities acting as
> landowners, financial institutions providing funds and developers with
> their technical and market expertise.[38]

The large-scale capitalist producers' demand for realisation proved
insatiable. The reconstruction of town centres to service their
needs could not advance quickly enough for them so they began to
construct on the outskirts of traditional towns, in embryonic form,
the beginnings of their vision of the perfect city, a Utopia of shopping in which capitalist realisation would become a pure dream.

37 Nigel Dubben and Sarah Sayce, *Property Portfolio Management*, 1991
38 Ibid.

The first tentative manifestation of this was the 'superstore', a massive outlet for a single retailer conglomerate. For property investors,

> superstore is a generic name to cover large single stores, constructed on greenfield sites in edge-of-town or out-of-town locations. They have evolved as a natural progression from the town centre supermarket ... the design of superstores has also undergone rapid development from early structures of almost industrial design, to an extensively landscaped and aesthetically sympathetic [design].[39]

Superstores were soon grouping themselves together to form 'retail parks'. But these represented merely the skeletal assembly of what was to become the true precursor of the pure realisation environment. In order to achieve this the social element of cities needed to be extracted, homogenised and alienated so that it could be incorporated into the retail park. This social element was leisure.

The alienation of leisure started with the construction of 'leisure parks', standard edge-of-town warehouse-park units identical in format to the retail parks. Leisure parks became the warehouse depots supplying urban areas with 'leisure', that is privatised leisure consumption. Privatised leisure is any leisure activity which can be profitably fitted into a shed – a cinema, a nightclub, a fast-food restaurant, etc. All of these activities are homogenised in form so that they can fit into packaged time periods and industrial warehouse spaces – leisure sheds can quickly be converted back into storage units if badly located.

This 'leisure property' of the property investment industry thus establishes in our minds the concept of leisure enclosure, leisure as the ticketed private property of a leisure company for which we

39 *Property Portfolio Management.*

must pay. We have no choice but to accept that we must purchase our own leisure time and that the content of our leisure is predetermined in shape and form for us by a property company and located by planners in specific leisure zones, heavily policed and usually situated out-of-town. At this point we are ready to accept the transformation of all of society external to the workplace into a single leisure shopping area.

Towards leisure discipline

Capitalism is fundamentally a society of consumption. Consumption rather than production is the defining action of bourgeois society because capitalism is owned by the bourgeoisie and they are a class of consumers, not producers. Their consumption, like their society, is hierarchical. The bourgeoisie can afford to consume goods which we are unable to buy. First among these is the ambrosia which regenerates their wealth, the content of our very lives as their workers.

The factory system is, in reality, a gigantic system for the consumption by the bourgeoisie of our daily lives We, as their workers, are forced to give them – the owners of the means of production – almost our entire lives.

From its outset then capitalism has been a system for determining and controlling the environment of consumption. First in the factories where the rich consume surplus labour time (virtually the whole working day), and then in society at large where they attempt to guarantee the conversion of surplus value into profit by making the purchase of their factory products unavoidable for us.

It is a grave vexation to capitalists that, while they have developed Taylorist sciences of discipline and control to force us to work in a regimented and predictable way they cannot scientifically force us to shop in the same manner.

This then is the next stage of bourgeois society simply explained, the creation of an environment in which the working class is controlled, channelled towards and then forced to purchase consumer commodities after work – a world of alienated leisure time as the perfect complement to our alienated labour time.

Consumerism: mass realisation

Just as the hand tools of pre-industrial workers reared up before them in vast industrialised forms, so now the urban environment of the quiet shopping high street has begun to rear up before us.

In the first era of industrialisation the town was centred around a factory producing primary goods: textiles, coal, steel, the materials for further industrialisation. Production was, for the most part, directed towards demand for these, some of which was coming from overseas colonial markets.

As industrial techniques caused food and other primary products to fall in price, manufacturers suffered a crisis of profitability. The market for these goods was saturating and the cost of meeting this saturation was now so low that there was little room for profit. Manufacturers responded by creating new consumer products incorporating immense waste and packaging.

Kelloggs pioneered this technique, applying it first among the corn farmers of 1890s America, producers who were the first to experience chronic devaluation due to the efficiency of mass over-production. By creating a 'health food' which discarded eighty per cent of the maize content and placed the remaining husk refuse in a huge cardboard packet, Kelloggs showed the way forward. Situated at the railhead of the midwest American corn-belt, Kelloggs' factory showed how capitalists could re-valorise their over-cheapened products by developing techniques of mass-wastage. Applied to all other subsequently devalued commodities, the even-

tual effect of this technique on the high streets of the Western
world has been dynamic.

The creation of the 'consumer good', a product aimed at consumption by workers themselves rather than by factories and transport systems in colonial markets, and characterised by wastage of
raw materials, advertising and packaging, has facilitated the re-
invention of the high street. Town streets have ceased to be drab
conveyor belts for workers to trudge along each day between bar-
rack-like housing and the factory. From the 1950s onwards, town
planners set about banishing industry from the centre of towns and
replacing it with retailing, commerce and luxury real estate (hotels
and managerial housing). The high street redesigned as a shopping
centre has ousted the factories, mines and foundries of the old
town centre as the new focus of urbanism.

First corner shops and livestock markets fell to the agglomerating effects of bank, retail and supermarket chains, primitively co-
ordinated into homogeneous high-street combinations by property
companies (the physical manifestations of finance capital).

But this 'formal subsumption of leisure under capital' – in
which capital seizes hold of the original corner shop and multi-
plies and enlarges it into an urban shopping centre – still caused
capitalism to experience a barrier to total realisation by the 1980s.
The drabness of capitalist environments had returned at a more
intense level.

> Financial institutions and pension funds bought up freeholds and raised
> rents [in town centres] to the point where only the strong or the multiples
> could survive. Britain's main high streets all looked virtually identical – a
> dreary procession of building societies and retail chains … the theory
> behind the 'leisure shopping' concept – and one of the biggest problems
> which faced retailers – was that consumers who did have money were
> bored [with capitalism].

REPETITIVE FAME INJURY

a low-waged economy filled
with self-employed clowns
competing with each other
to be "famous" at late-night
corporate events

'There's not just a standardised range of products now, there's a standardised range of shops selling them. There's a high degree of predictability, so the shopping centres have got to have something else to induce people to go there' ... the target became transforming shopping from a chore into a full-scale leisure activity.[40]

The total recomposition of the town centre since the 1940s into a more efficient realisation environment for recouping profits from commodity production was therefore only a prelude. The full revolutionisation of the entire concept of the town has seen capitalism take the first tentative steps towards creating an environment of pure realisation; the town as a vast machine of purified shopping with the social elements of the traditional town (housing, education, local political representation, etc.) substituted by a single, anaemic, pseudo-social element – 'leisure and entertainment'. Thus is produced the pseudo-socialising atmosphere of intensified shopping.

This transition from the formal to the 'real' subsumption of leisure under capital (society as socially exclusive leisure shopping) arrives with the creation of the phenomenon variously termed the 'regional shopping complex', the 'large-scale' or 'out-of-town shopping centre' or, most commonly, the 'mega-mall'.

Mega-malls

With the advent of the mega-mall the retail park and the leisure park combine to form a new dialectical urbanism which abolishes nearby towns, as a property investment analyst illustrates:

The true out-of-town shopping centre [mega-mall] aims to provide the

40 'A Nation of Shoppers', *Observer Magazine*, 13 December 1992.

full range of products and services that are associated with the town centre. Not only will a full range of retail goods be found, but also services such as banks, creche, cafe and, typically, leisure facilities such as health [fitness] centre and cinema.

It will have a retail floor area in excess of 100,000 square metres and extensive car parking ... it can be seen, therefore, that the essential ingredients are the same as for town centres; the difference lies in the scale of the development and the amount of leisure and associated facilities provided, many of which would not be viable as independent developments but whose costs are justified because the presence of such facilities [increases] the time each shopper spends in the centre and thus the 'unit spend' is increased, and hence profitability ... the mega-mall is still embryonic in most cases.[41]

With the opening of West Edmonton Mall in Canada in 1984 and subsequent mega-malls in the USA and Britain, the barrier of shopping restricted to an urban setting acting as a restraint to the pure mass-realisation of surplus value has finally been broken.

This Cyclopean shopping environment has the effect of literally abolishing nearby town centres, sucking out towards itself the central shopping principle of neighbouring towns and cities and leaving behind a husk of social deprivation (this is termed the 'doughnut effect' in America after the 1970s' experience of cities such as Detroit, where the exodus of manufacturing industry, followed by the abolition of its replacement, down-town shopping centres, left an urban ring of decaying housing clustered around an extinct city centre).

Suddenly imploded town centres, derelict and crime-ridden, are left behind by the car-driving majority who can afford to live away from the run-down ghettos of the 'unconsuming' and unemployed;

41 *Property Portfolio Management.*

just as the first urban workers left behind the destitute peasants on the land in the first wave of industrialisation.

The impact of mega-malls

The mega-mall is not simply a huge department store, it is a shopping DisneyWorld, a theme park in which the 'theme' is the perfect capitalist society. At present the world contains very few mega-malls; only a handful exist in the USA, Canada, Britain (MetroCentre, Meadowhall, Bluewater, etc.), and Japan. Their impact is titanic and immediate, however. The opening of the MetroCentre on a 'greenfield site' near Gateshead in northern England immediately 'abolished' Gateshead's town centre, leaving it derelict and boarded up as shops migrated out or failed to compete.

The shock of American-style urban decay appearing so instantly in Britain – where it had been assumed that such decay was the culmination of specific social processes taking decades rather than the result of a capitalist process taking a handful of weeks from the opening of a mega-mall – produced the 'town-centre management movement' amongst British planners.

At present further development of mega-malls in Britain is suspended but the genie is out of the flask, the town-centre management movement is lost in a hopeless dialectic with the mega-malls. It is striving to protect traditional town centres from their onslaught simply by converting town centres into privatised mega-mall replicas. The town-centre management movement in the UK is therefore a further part of the logic of the mega-mall, the transition of the formal to the real subsumption of leisure under capital.

The mega-mall as the beginnings of real subsumption of leisure under capital

The mega-mall (and any town centre remodelled to mimic it) combines all the elements of the property-company-inspired high-street template and revolutionises them.

Instead of the traditional post-war town-centre mix of various high-street commercial units owned by competing property companies and operated by competing national and regional shopping chains, the mega-mall is owned, designed, constructed and managed from the outset by property developers and huge retail corporations working together because they are all subsidiary companies of global investors. They are set up at out-of-town locations in opposition to cities which they aim to replace and are governed by unelected managers. Supermarkets, banks, department stores and boutique chains which have all previously been features of homogenised high streets now merge together to form just part of the content of the mega-mall.

The mega-mall is an adventure for the privileged shopper. Like a holiday, it is accessed by car. Like capitalist society, of which it is the highest expression, its ideology is one of comforting safety. It proudly displays the fact that it is policed by security patrols and surveyed by cameras, it hints that its 'out-of-town location' is beyond the reach of the non-car-owning destitute, there are no graffiti and no homeless sleeping in doorways (in fact there is no concept of sleep in a mega-mall).

The mega-mall is totally privatised. Its only civic culture is its leisure areas, fun rides, arcades and fast-food 'grazing space' for the spellbound shopper. Enclosed and brightly lit, it is a timeless place of endless shopping, simultaneously a frenetic hive and an awesome neon cathedral.

The mega-mall is a physical advert for the act of shopping itself, but shopping as a leisure activity, in fact shopping as an exciting replacement for leisure. Like society rebuilt as a Cyclopean computer game, the mega-mall offers itself to the worker as the enchanted 'highest level' where the successful player can 'download their accumulated credits'. Shoppers are invited to wander at will, to create their own maps, to get lost in the deliberately confusing layout of the mega-mall.

With the mega-mall, capitalism instinctively adopts elements of the revolutionary critique of political economy developed by the 1960s workers' movement (the situationists). Their concept of 'derive', a free, unplanned urbanism of free individuals drifting through a city of self-made adventures, has become the adventure of drifting through a subliminally programmed environment of hyper-consumption.

> Retailing analysts say the apparent 'confusion' of different routes and choices of direction is carefully built into many mega-malls to give jaded consumers the 'excitement' of exploration. 'Even if they get lost its no bad thing … as long as they can find their way back ultimately, the fact they get lost means they pass more shops.'[42]

The layout of the mega-mall transmits its encoded dictatorship of consumption behaviour to the consumer as scientifically as the production line controls the worker at work. And just like the automated factory, the impact of the mega-mall is socially revolutionary. It forces towns (which have in any case been rapidly deindustrialising in preparation for their abolition as centres organised around the principle of industrial labour rather than industrialised consumption) to remodel themselves as mega-malls or perish.

42 *A Nation of Shoppers.*

C

Leisure planning

In response to the 'challenge' of the mega-mall, town planners banish the remaining industrial units from their centres and rebuild them around leisure and shopping. Town planning is revolutionised into the industrialised science of leisure shopping. An incredibly sophisticated 'micro-Haussmanist' architecture is now created.[43] Main streets are meticulously replanned by architects, businessmen and police advisers working together to produce a perfect capitalist high street just as in a mega-mall.

These new high streets are designed to confuse the pedestrian into wandering past as many shops as possible, to make shopping areas appear exciting and to allow for the rapid, unobtrusive deployment of security snatch squads. Streets are pedestrianised to allow uninterrupted street-length vistas for security-camera surveillance and seemingly innocent items of street furniture such as plant pots, banners and fountains are strategically placed as both psychological reinforcements of the leisure theme and obstructions to ram-raiders and escaping shoplifters. Security, pedestrianisation and anti-graffiti patrols combine to reproduce the privatisation of public space intrinsic to the environment of a private mega-mall.

In this way the creation of the mega-mall sets up a Darwinistic dialectic. It forces all the nearby towns to successfully remodel their centres in the exact likeness of a mega-mall or be extinguished. This dialectic is the start of the real subsumption of leisure under capital.

The business interests in each town (increasingly the same global investors) install an unelected civic dictator, the 'town-

---

43 Haussman was commissioned by Napoleon to redesign Paris so that rioters could be dispersed by cavalry charges down clear, straight avenues rather than the warren of back streets which had previously aided their escape.

centre manager', to co-ordinate the transformation of urban zones into private shopping areas for them and to banish the poor from their streets. Standing above these new managers is the co-ordinating role of the state which now attempts to criminalise all leisure activities not oriented around corporate shopping. Thus even the Glastonbury (Shopping) Festival can become a state-sanctioned 'temporary town centre' under its unelected farmer-manager.

But no matter how much of an impresario the private centre manager attempts to be, capitalism can never succeed in preventing ever-greater levels of boredom arising in response to its shoddy, profit-farmed world of choiceless and hierarchical leisure-shopping. It therefore has to use legislation to make shopping discipline compulsory.

Non-shopping leisure becomes 'pirate leisure time'. Crime and the usage of leisure time by the underclass become the fixations of the national government and mass media ('zero tolerance') as the destitute are progressively isolated from successful town centres as effectively as they are from the private mega-mall. Architecture merges with policing, transport planning and media to create on earth the 'heaven' of the television advertisers.

The whole of society outside work becomes a leisure shopping area until consumption is fully intensified and society revolutionised into a pure leisure shopping environment, an endless, unavoidable advert for the realisation of surplus value. In this way advertising and urbanism are transcended as capitalism controls our environment against us to force us to consume its empty, pre-packaged substitute for the content of our entire lives – the 'lifestyle'.

'Lifestyle' and cybernetic shopping

The 'lifestyle' is the totally constructed image of life that faultlessly marries together all the reciprocally supporting joists of the capitalist advertiser's dystopia. The ideal consumer is depicted as living in a comfortable high-value apartment requiring continuous replenishment with further consumer items (implying that house-price-threatening crime outside has been crushed).

This consumer is eternally young, implying endless access to disposable income, is permanently fascinated with new cars, instinctively hates the working class who are viewed only as dangerous street people to be insulated against, and knows how to avoid boredom by belief in gigantic, hyped-up consumer events. In short, the 'lifestyle' is projected by advertisers as the off-the-peg human software for workers to install (as an aspiration, regardless of how distant it may be from their ability to pay) in order to be able to tolerate the leisure shopping environment of the mega-mall outside.[44]

'Convenience', the term for the passive acceptance of these pre-designed pseudo-choices, and the maintenance of a high income are the key themes of this software package not only in adverts but in most characteristic television programmes, in the news, in the mass media and in leisure environments themselves.

So, following this logic and eclipsing even the mega-mall in terms of intensive shopping as well as introducing the most purely proletarianised office work yet witnessed under capitalism is the phenomenon of the 'call centre'.

The facilities for the paltry supply of credit and debt to workers,

---

44 Those few who can afford to reject the lifestyle in its standard form (and consume instead the unimaginatively entitled, but equally expensive, 'alternative lifestyle') are currently being courted as circus entertainment to 'enliven' mega-mall environments. The British state wrote off millions on behalf of its capitalists to research this possibility at its mega-mall laboratory – The Millennium Dome.

enabling us to carry out our duty of consuming after work, are increasingly evaporating from the high street to reappear as telephone call centres, vast human battery farms employing low-paid workers living outside the 'lifestyle' in derelict areas abandoned by both mega-malls and town-centre management. They work under total surveillance, chained to telephones and computers which churn out acoustic and repetitive strain injuries by the hour. These 24-hour banking centres now employ two per cent of the British workforce (half a million people) in office conditions reminiscent of early industrial mills.

Advertisers dream further that, because of these intensive inputting centres, even the mega-malls will eventually evaporate to be replaced by shopping via networked computers, a world in which all shopping will be conducted through global Internet links to vast call-centres and distribution warehouses.

The aspiration is that each consumer will, from their armchairs, use the Internet to engage in global arbitrage to obtain by mail order the cheapest individual goods from any intensive, low-waged warehouse complex or factory outlet on earth (rather than travelling to a shop to buy them). This demonstrates that, whether they are being realistic or not, capitalists are envisaging a more profound upheaval for our world than any working-class revolutionary dares to speculate about, while actively plotting a society more gruesomely proletarianised than any working-class revolutionary dreads to imagine.

Globalisation of the factory system

How is it possible for capitalism to reinvent city centres around consumption rather than around production? It is cities, after all, into which peasants are driven in order to separate them from the land and force them to accept the factory system. How then can

MACHINES DO ALL THE WORK
SO THAT WE CAN GET R.S.I.

industrial capitalism remove the industrial principle from its city centres and hope to survive?

The answer is simple. The factory is the scientifically designed system through which the bourgeoisie can extract the maximum amount of surplus value for the lowest possible price. The factory is a only system; it need not be a system of manufacturing production. Any form of productive labour can be regimented:

> ... for instance, Milton, who wrote *Paradise Lost*, was an unproductive worker. On the other hand, a writer who turns out work for his publisher in a factory style is a productive worker ... to be a productive worker is therefore not a piece of luck but a misfortune.[45]

There is no more reason why the factory must remain restricted to being a centre of purely industrial manufacturing production any more than there was for original, nineteenth-century industrial equipment to be restricted purely to farming.

Just as peasant agriculture was swept away by early capitalism and replaced with an industrialised form of farming using heavy machinery and few workers, so today manufacturing and heavy industry are in turn being cleared away from the West's city centres and removed on a global scale to more marginal areas of the planet away from the dominant economic nations.

This is simply a prelude to the total robotisation of manufacturing. As few people will need to be employed within this sphere in the future as are now employed in mechanised farming (where once almost the entire working population of nations was concentrated). Manufacturing production will follow the same path as agricultural production which increased exponentially during the twentieth century while employing fewer and fewer workers.

45 *Capital.*

Manufactured goods will rapidly become as cheap to make as farm produce (i.e. almost uneconomical). The need to revalorise their deflated investments through realisation will mean that the leading economic nations will come to be dominated by leisure consumption, mass employment in the 'service sector' in other words. For this to occur the diversity of service provision must be homogenised by the bourgeoisie and brought within the factory system. To do this the bourgeoisie is developing the cybernetic revolution.

Cybernetic capitalism: the subsumption of Fordism

Because the society of the real subsumption of leisure under capital is one of intensified consumption, it has to be one of intensified proletarianisation. Cybernetics, correctly identified by the most advanced sections of the workers' movement of the 1960s as the next phase of proletarianisation, is the central method being used to re-regiment the workplace and enable the factory system to extend into hitherto inaccessible areas.

Networked computers reproduce a highly hierarchical system of control over the labour process which exactly replicates, complements and intensifies the in-built hierarchical control of previous industrial technology. Through networked computers, managerial control, monitoring and surveillance of production speed is now instantaneous. Cybernetics brings whole swathes of formerly skilled labour within the scope of the factory system.

Computer technology allows workers to manipulate sophisticated equipment using ever more basic and transferable skills. Computer software homogenises production by interposing a layer of operational instructions between workers and equipment. The ease with which this software (as opposed to the machinery it is linked to) can be operated enables each worker to become interchangeable. Widely differing production techniques, which would formerly have required specialist basic training to perform, come to be controlled by a layer of computer software with commands increasingly similar to those used by the software packages controlling all other fields of production and which can quickly be taught to any new worker.

Gradually all production turns into office administration work and the factory becomes limitless. Workers operate equipment far away or are thoroughly isolated from each other by being made to work from home, hierarchically linked together by telecommunications. With the advent of cybernetics a 'factory floor' can span the entire globe. The 'farming out' of data processing within even medium-sized firms hunting the globe for the cheapest packages of labour is becoming commonplace in all industrialised countries.

In short, cybernetics is the software to convert the entire world into a single factory to be dialectically integrated with its illusory opposition, the endless leisure shopping environment. What other dream could capitalist society have for itself?

House prices relative to house
ratios

6

5

1983 1986 1989 199

ndon
rth
thern Ireland
st Midlands

**Consternation breaks out
at the Stock Exchange
when Hegel predicts the
future of house prices**

CONTESTING UNCLE GEORGE'S WILL

All the theoretical strands of the revolutionary workers' movement stem from critical confrontation with Hegelian thought. (Guy Debord)

Hegel: the Moses of the pyramid scheme

Having analysed the continuing revolutionary nature of bourgeois society as it embarks on the next stage of its social transformation, we now turn to its need to defend itself against its own negation.

Capitalist society is an ongoing revolution predicated on the mass creation of an integrated global proletariat. In other words, capitalism can only continue by increasing the numbers of exploited workers, by training us, by politicising us, by linking us together in increasingly interdependent coalitions (the factory system), by constantly raising up and organising an unhappy opposition to its own activities. The principle product of the capitalist system is an ever-larger working class or, from capitalism's point of view, an ever-cheaper source of the 'magical royal jelly' it extracts from each worker – surplus value.

We, the proletariat created by capitalism, are increasingly unable to find any effective means to protect ourselves from exploitation, and from the shoddy world built for us to facilitate that exploitation, other than through totally overthrowing the capitalist system. As the proletariat we quickly learn that our attempts to use the logic of political economy (the science of capitalism) in our defence are doomed.

Following the theory of equitable commodity exchange expounded by political economy, we workers at first band together into trades unions in an attempt to drive up the price of our labour as a commodity. This action is as swiftly smashed by capitalism as are all other attempts artificially to increase the costs of its raw materials, be they inaccessible highways, trading tariffs, producer cartels or physical walls.

The failure of trades unions to defend workers within the capitalist system forces us to abandon political economy as a source of defence and to begin theorising our situation, in other words to begin to form a revolutionary theory. This is the point at which we begin the 'critique of political economy' that forces us to engage with the theories of revolution developed by bourgeois society for itself.

The foremost bourgeois philosopher of revolution (and the ultimate justifier of its private-property system) is Georg Wilhelm Friedrich Hegel (1770–1831), and it is with Hegel that the workers' movement begins the theoretical critique of bourgeois society.

[Bourgeois] Philosophers are doomed to find Hegel waiting patiently at the end of whatever road we travel. (Rorty).

The theory of bourgeois revolution

Hegel's philosophy is the canonical text of the bourgeois revolution. Hegel is the booming prophet who justifies the 'revolution from above' and who eulogises planning as divine. According to Hegel, the Mind of God is realised on earth as progressive history in the form of developing rational planning systems, the evolution of constitutional governments into strong nation-states (a modernising force sprung 'rationally' from the revolutionary overthrow of feudalism) and an everlasting respect for private-property ownership as the ultimate expression of human freedom.

It would be difficult to invent for the bourgeoisie a more convenient philosophy than that of Hegel. But self-satisfied as Hegel's system might at first appear it is riven with precisely the same contradiction as is bourgeois society itself. For Hegel interprets the free alienation of private property (the freedom to trade without feudal restrictions and duties) as the ultimate form of freedom. In doing so he opens up the terrible mechanism of political economy (the scientific study of bourgeois society) at the level of philosophy. Once set in motion this ticks inexorably towards its own critique because, in the bourgeoisie's free market, where property can be bought and sold without reference to its former owner, our working lives are traded as the most valuable property of all. By the impossible act of separating our 'labour time' from our real lives, the bourgeoisie alienates us into a commodity on its 'labour market'. And so we experience its ultimate form of freedom as a general condition of slavery.

This is why the philosophy of Hegel is the Achilles' heel of the bourgeoisie; he is at once its champion and its worst enemy.

The theory of democratic history

Hegel's bizarre view of history is essentially the theory of history democratised but then suspended prematurely before the implications of full democracy can be realised. In this way Hegel's theory of history is identical to the practice of bourgeois society itself.

Prior to Hegel, written history largely consisted of the biographies of kings and generals, and gossip surrounding their lives and sayings. The only 'purposes' revealed in these histories were the personal destinies of these great figures and the goals and means of achievement they used to fulfil them.

The concept of democracy was synonymous with that of anarchy. To allow the population of a nation to govern themselves was akin to allowing wild beasts to rule. The existence of a rudimentary democracy in Switzerland was distrusted but seen as an anomaly attributed to mountain life (even so Switzerland was attacked by many neighbouring kingdoms to 'bring order' to its chaos).

As feudal history – like feudal society – did not accept a concept of democracy as anything other than chaos, it did not acknowledge any notion of a destiny for the human race as a whole except to assist the rise of hereditary kingship. When populations featured in these histories at all their lives appeared only as the raw material for great kings to mould into their personal destiny. Races and nations were supposed to be composed only of recalcitrant potential soldiers (and wild enemies) whose historical role was to have their cowardice drummed out of them on the battlefield in order to help realise the genius of a great monarch through conquest and triumph.

The highest social expression early historians were capable of conveying was the notion of a triumphant nation, which owed its power to the fortunate and wise guidance of a great hereditary dynasty. Because of this, history before Hegel contained no concept of evolution. The nearest it came was the concept of genealogy, or the ascendant breeding of great families.

Hegel did not invent the concept of historical evolution however; he was merely forced by events to democratise genealogy. When this hereditary principle is extended to the whole human race it becomes the theory of evolution. Though the upward

Chipmunk-faced miser Warren Buffett buys us all a television, just like the one he got his struggling daughter when he abandoned her in Washington.

progress of great families might come to an end through a lack of offspring or financial ruin, an end to the upward progress of the 'great family' of the human race would require extinction.

And so evolution was bound to be a progressive concept since it explained the economic growth which had emerged from the late Middle Ages onwards. The rich began to expect their family's wealth to grow over generations thanks to the benefits of the enclosures – the agglomeration of farms – they were carrying out.

The life of a patriarch of a great family was assessed according to how well he had progressed his family name, whether or not he had managed to preserve the estate he inherited while bequeathing a greater one to his children. The democratised version of this expectation of an endlessly accumulating wealth was the concept of the evolution of humanity as a whole.

Humanity was seen to be similarly progressing towards a greater glory, but in this case a universal one. In this way the notion of human evolution is not one of static reproduction but of dynamic expansion. Democratic history therefore has a Utopian goal called 'Progress'. But the transition from a concept of progressive genealogy (the expanding wealth of aristocratic families) to a more democratic concept of progressive evolution (the expanding wealth of humanity) is not philosophical but revolutionary.

This is because the process that makes great families richer is precisely that which impoverishes a growing number of the rest of humanity. As humanity grows richer it is only already wealthy families that enjoy the benefits until a revolutionary challenge is mounted against this process by the dispossessed.

Hegel and revolution

It was the French Revolution that forced Hegel to widen the traditional focus of history outwards from the individualised study of great families and dynastically ruled nations to include the democratic notion of a whole human race striving towards a universal historic goal. The vanity that maintained that history was the personal prerogative of aristocratic families was violently shattered when scores of them were sent to the guillotine by the mob in France in the 1790s. But, as the revolutionary masses forced their way on to the stage of history, they did not succeed in establishing the total universal democracy they demanded.

As we have already seen, the people who seized control of the new post-revolutionary society were not the population as a unified whole but one ascendant class of it – the bourgeoisie, the first revolutionary class ever to win.

The bourgeoisie acknowledged the people's calls for 'democracy, liberty and fraternity' and bowed to their demands to form rational republics in France and America. But they had no intention of allowing the future to become the seething triumph of a revolutionary mob.

For the bourgeoisie, as for the revolutionary masses from which they were emerging, history had a democratic purpose and an evolutionary principle of growth. But these notions of democracy and evolution were to remain subservient to their interests, their collective accumulation of private property. This still made the bourgeoisie more democratic than the aristocracy in the sense that their interests were broader class interests rather than family interests.

History did not cease to be the genealogy of great families in order to become the full democratic history of the human race. Only half of this development has so far been achieved. History has become the collective history of bourgeois interest and evolution the evolution of the bourgeoisie's 'estate', their profitable investments referred to collectively as 'economic growth'.

Hegelian theory of revolution

Hegel theorises the triumph of the bourgeoisie who, while adopting the rhetoric of universal democracy, only believe in the democracy of their own victory. In order to explain the arrival of democracy through the impact of revolution, Hegel was compelled to explain evolution as being revolutionary; he could hardly explain it any other way in the light of events.

To do this Hegel developed the theory of the dialectic, and in doing so revealed that his theory (like the new bourgeois society it theorised) was redolent with the threat of future revolution.

The dialectic is the movement of history towards universal democracy. This movement is not transcendental but antagonistic; over aeons of time the victims of oppression struggle to gain their freedom from those who are oppressing them. This movement starts with the 'oppression' of a hostile natural world in which human beings are uniquely ill-equipped to survive. They have therefore to struggle to gain mastery over an alien environment. From this point onwards groups of people seek mastery over other groups by seeing in them the same alienation they have experienced in nature and by enslaving them as they have the elements of the natural world.

Thus the world divides into oppressors and oppressed, with the oppressed forming their oppressor's 'negation' in their struggle to overcome them. But in overcoming oppression the oppressed go on to form a higher system of oppression themselves from which further struggle (negation) emerges against them.

Through this repetitive process, higher and higher stages of oppression and freedom are achieved which synthesise into a higher and more rational form of human consciousness. Finally, the human race achieves its goal of total freedom and rationality with freedom from oppression by natural forces and total democracy.

Because this is a process of evolution, Hegel sees human history as the original struggle between oppressor and oppressed repeated over and over again, each time raised up to a higher historical level but carrying all the elements of all the previous levels subsumed within it. These levels are 'realised', or made sense of, only within the context of the latest level to incorporate them.

This view of history as an ever-greater telescoping of all previous antagonistic moments Hegel termed 'totality'. Just as the revolutionary masses who stormed the Bastille did not suddenly assemble out of nowhere but had been gathering to destroy the French aristocracy for some time, so the negation in Hegel's system is the potential for the oppressed to seek revolution as well as the action of revolution itself.

Thus Hegel's theory of negation is a theory of revolutionary potential but, despite having revolutionary potential as its driving force, his philosophy is ultimately conservative.

Hegel believed that the struggle of oppressor against oppressed had reached its highest expression in his own times as the struggle of revolutionary nations striving to abolish feudalism and establish modern liberal democratic states, exemplified by his own state of Prussia. Although revolutionary France had been the instigator of European modernisation under the conquering direction of Napoleon Bonaparte, Prussia, Hegel maintained, was the final synthesised totality of all previous revolutionary struggles and counter-balancing reactions. The history he theorised as having been dynamically revolutionary had now come to an end. According to Hegel we are not living in a period of limbo between an alienated, slave society and a self-consciously free society; we are living in 1819!

Hegel theorised that with the promulgation of a new constitution for the Prussian state in which he was living in 1819 (a bourgeois constitutional monarchy), history had come to an end and the rational perfection he had anticipated as a result of the dialectic had arrived, or at least humanity was as self-consciously free as it could ever hope to be.

The end of history had resulted in a comfortable, bourgeois state with an industrialising economy surrounded by similar European nations.

Hegel's bizarre termination of revolutionary history – coming to an abrupt halt like a horse refusing its final fence – just as it reaches the advent of bourgeois society, is entirely in keeping with his role as the theorist of the bourgeois revolution. The problem is that by trying to incorporate into its triumph bourgeois society's revolutionary origins, the theory implies that this society will itself be overthrown.

It was not Hegel's task to explore the future of the dialectic. This task falls to us, the working class.

Hegelian contradictions for the bourgeoisie

The problem of Hegel is not some dry academic debate of little relevance to modern revolutionaries; it is of vital importance. We live within the on-going revolution of bourgeois society, a society which sets as its goal the total transformation of society into an integrated factory system and the complete unification of the human race within that global system of production for profit. The theorist used to justify this revolutionary mission is Hegel.

The work of Hegel endorses capitalism as a society of constant revolutionary change based on private property ownership. More than Locke and Hobbes before him, he is *the* theorist of revolutionary leasehold landlordism (the revolt by shopkeepers against the feudal freehold owners of their shops). He defines it as the forward march of Progress, the spiritual uplifting of humanity until the political triumph of these self-liberating shop-owners merges with the Mind of God!

Capitalism has never seriously attempted to replace Hegel's work with a more modern theory of revolution precisely because it does not require a more modern revolution to take place (a revolution by workers, tenants and customers for instance).

Paradoxically, bourgeois society seeks to present itself as a system of comforting stability and predictable normality. But because it originates illegitimately with the wholesale theft of feudal land, and operates by creating within itself a massively alienated working class, the ultimate destination of the bourgeois revolution is anything but predictable. It is intensely ambiguous, and therefore so too is the conservativism of the Hegelian thinking used to justify it.

Relying on Hegel to serve as a timeless endorsement for its system is as dangerous for bourgeois society as is the everyday practice of its very existence. Bourgeois society is acutely aware that in furthering its revolution it is simultaneously raising up its own negation in the form of a gigantic working class.

For this working class to critically explore the revolutionary method of Hegel in order to justify its attack on capitalism, to use the highest language of capitalism against it, is a potentially lethal development for bourgeois society. For this reason bourgeois thinkers have spent the past century and a half attempting the impossible task of trying to remove the revolutionary potential from Hegel, as futile a task as that of their masters as they simultaneously try to remove the social revolutionary potential from capitalist society itself.

The recurrent end of history

Like all bourgeois philosophers, the current triumphalist philosopher of capitalism is an Hegelian. In *The End of History and the Last Man* (1992), Francis Fukuyama offers afresh the ruling class's recurrent theory of history as the globalisation of capitalism, arguing that with the collapse of the Soviet Bloc the liberal democratic market economy has become the last remaining universal ideology and therefore not an ideology at all but the end of history itself.

From now on we shall be living in 1989 forever instead of 1819![46] Through struggle the human race has finally arrived at the globalisation of the American way as its final truth and goal. Revolution has become the presence of a Gap store and Macdonalds in every town and every true revolutionary should be rushing to work there.

By producing this theory, bourgeois society has reminded us of its unending loyalty to Hegel, whose dynamic and evolving theory of history always appears to have just ended with the triumph of the status quo whenever we look at it.

The need to prevent the working class from appropriating the revolutionary possibilities in the work of Hegel has meant that the 'deconstruction' of Hegel (who's thought forms the basis of modern terms such as 'philosophy', 'theory', 'history', and 'grand narrative') has been the prerequisite for being accepted as a bourgeois theorist for decades.

The very term deconstruction explains the delicate task of stripping down Hegelian thought during periods of worker militancy and removing its revolutionary possibilities while maintaining it in a form still employable by the bourgeoisie – leaving a 'post-structure' devoid of revolutionary potential. But the instant bourgeois society feels confident enough to proclaim itself once more the ultimate revolutionary movement of all time (that is, the instant it feels the threat of proletarian revolution is in abeyance) it immedi-

---

46 Fukuyama continues to demonstrate his inability to conceive of a proletarian revolution by stating at a conference (otherwise correctly) that capitalism cannot collapse as a system even if it collapses economically. *Independent on Sunday*, 6 December 1998.

ately reconstructs Hegel. Capitalism simultaneously maintains the legacy of Hegel as its self-glorification while attempting to neuter it whenever that legacy becomes a threat.

Refutation of Hegel during confrontational periods

For as long as Hegelian method has been taken up as a critical weapon by the working class, Hegel has been the special subject of every counter-revolutionary philosopher. For years these specialists dedicated their volumes to disproving Hegel and, by implication, the entire Enlightenment project. Fear of what workers could fashion from Hegel (beginning with their theorist Karl Marx) prompted the counter-revolutionary philosophers to argue that the notions of progress and totality in Hegel's work were meaningless and that history and humanity were non-existent.

The concept of progressive history as developing human consciousness is the bedrock of revolutionary theory. By deconstructing history (or announcing the 'end of history') bourgeois theorists believed they could abolish the possibility of proletarian revolution.

No one is suggesting that a theoretical termination of Hegelianism would suddenly cause the world's population to become passive and contented. Certainly revolutionary uprisings continue to take place as they have throughout history (we, the masses simply refuse to pore over the vanity publications of our betters, the reactionary professors, and accept that the age of revolution has been successfully deconstructed!). But it is the state's profound hope that if future revolutions can be divorced from a revolutionary theory of history then they can be portrayed as being nothing more than greater or lesser acts of vandalism by armed rabbles or mafia (organised shoplifting gangs).

We have already seen these calumnies against revolutionary proletarian consciousness levelled against a revolution in Albania in

1997, a revolt itself dismissed as a mafia uprising when, in reality, it was sparked by a wholesale attack on a mafia state by revolutionary workers. Doubtless further workers' revolts will be attributed to orchestration by drug-dealers or speculators.

The reactionary professors are currently free to insult workers in this way because radical theorists have abandoned Hegelian analysis to their bourgeois enemies in the state universities and media. The ending of the cold war has witnessed bourgeois theorists in Western universities flocking to restore Hegel to the mantleshelves of their tearooms. Suddenly all their postmodern misgivings seem to have disappeared. While the proletarian cat is asleep these bourgeois mice can play with Hegel to their hearts' content.

They do not of course raise a revolutionary critique of Hegel. Instead they resurrect Hegel as he was in 1819. Yet again they have conveniently rediscovered Hegel at the very moment when history has come to an end! Academics in the service of the ruling classes find as much comfort in lauding Hegel when the workers' movement is in abeyance as they find need to discredit him when his theory is seized upon by us as the key to unlocking capitalism's secret, the secret that it is weaving the global judo mat upon which the world's workers can overthrow it.

Hegel was not a revolutionary theorist but a theorist of revolution. He was a conservative Christian philosopher and it is Hegel's dynamic theory of history, a theory forced upon him by the world's first truly historical revolution, the French Revolution, which makes it so necessary for revolutionaries to address Hegel's legacy.

In no way should Hegel be thought of as some difficult genius whose work must be understood in order to be a proper revolutionary. We must never lose sight of the fact that his revolution in thought came not from him but from the French revolutionary masses. It was their genius in proclaiming a rational republic that forced Hegel to theorise their actions.

The global spirit of history (the 'world soul')

Hegel's theory is of the bourgeois revolution having triumphed. Uncritiqued, it sustains that moment of triumph over feudalism forever, continuously re-glorifying the bourgeois revolution's victory up to whatever point it has currently reached. If trades unions unnaturally resurrect phantom figures such as guild-masters to do battle with, then the bourgeoisie continues to try thrilling us with tales of its latest courageous struggle with a long-dead aristocratic ruling class.

As the original political expressions of the bourgeois revolution were nationalism and colonialism, so Hegel theorises the historical struggle of people towards their total freedom as being embodied by the struggle of nations and empires. The struggle is directed by the heroic individual able to translate this popular will into his or her personal glory.

It is only the revolutionary workers' movement that can correct this error by demonstrating that the true struggle of human history is not between nations but between classes with the proletarian class consisting entirely of heroic individuals able through solidarity to embody our own popular will. We do this by engaging with the bourgeoisie to become the negation of the entire class system.

Bourgeois Hegelian manifestoes of the twentieth century therefore include Hitler's *Mein Kampf*, arguing as it does for Germany, under a revolutionary man of history, to struggle with other nations for the control of the world and thence the freedom of the German people.

Hegel was the original eulogiser of the revolutionary nationalist leader. He had witnessed Napoleon on the battlefield and had seen in him the embodiment of the historical mission of revolutionary France, to sweep away all the feudal institutions of Old Europe and modernise the world rationally through conquest:

> I saw the Emperor – that Global Spirit of History – riding out to
> reconnoitre the city. It is truly a wonderful sensation to see such an
> individual, concentrated here on a single point, astride a horse, yet
> reaching across the world and ruling it.

What bourgeois leader or businessman, from Hitler to the monopoly capitalists of the present day, has ever been able to resist seeing
themselves as Hegel's final 'Spirit of History' personified or 'World
Soul', modernising the world and thereby ending history as their
own personal triumph?

The nightmare possibility remains that a world bourgeois revolution will occur which raises up such a world soul to the level of a
global Hitler, carried aloft by monopoly capitalists in order to
establish world government and cartelise the entire planet on their
behalf. Our salvation will arrive when the direction of history
ceases to be interpreted as the will of a single bourgeois individual
such as this (a latter-day Napoleon) but is personified instead as
the collective will of an entire revolutionary class. It will arrive
when we the proletariat become Hegel's Global Spirit of History.

Hegel deconstructed

Bourgeois society is stalled theoretically at the level of Hegel for
the simple reason that we are stalled at the level of bourgeois society. This is why Hegel is endlessly deconstructed and rebuilt by
reactionary politicians and theorists.

In the twentieth century, each time that a burgeoning workers'
movement formed a revolutionary critique of Hegel (by forming a
revolutionary critique of bourgeois society on the streets) capitalism's toy-dog academics have yapped into battle to kill the revolutionary dragon on paper! Furiously they sterilise Hegel (even
attempting to refute him during particularly threatening periods)

as if this dry theorising can set adrift any revolutionary gains by the working class.

All the post-structuralist nonsense to have emerged from the universities over the past thirty years is nothing more than the choirboys of the bourgeoisie singing hymns of praise to their attack on workers. It is merely Nietzsche's original critique of Hegel, recasting the concept of totality as an anaemic series of empty, elitist recurrences, repeated at a professionalised level by an anaemic elite of unoriginal professors as bourgeois writers have attempted to exorcise the spectre of 1968.

Now they believe that the spectre is back in its grave, bourgeois society has instantly reinstated Hegel, its flawed revolutionary prophet, on his plinth. Each new revolutionary uprising which attempts the 'abolition of all existing classes in a way that does not bring about a new division of society' tarnishes Hegel's statue in the eyes of the bourgeoisie. Such levels of contestation by the working class are currently returning.

Nationalism

As we have seen with Hegel, the dream of bourgeois society is of an heroic struggle of nations for global supremacy. This is the actual nightmare of capitalist domination opiated into a public fantasy. Bourgeois society requires its populations to be galvanised into revolutionary action behind the dynamic concept of 'their' struggling nation. Only the nation can guarantee the security of private property ownership (no matter how huge its scale) and can co-ordinate the planning, military power, policing and mass media needed to ensure a convivial environment for capitalists. Only the nation can act effectively to compartmentalise the world's proletariat, trapping us into the illusion of being separated into rival populations while international capitalists are free to act against us as a global class.

It is at the moment when we, the working class, begin our revo-lutionary dialectic with that global class, the point at which the revolutionary struggle between nations dissolves to reveal the rev-olutionary struggle between classes lying beneath it, that Hegelian theory, like a Grimm fairytale, begins to shift from its magical and comforting beginning towards its sinister and terrifying conclusion for the capitalist class.

The only possible transcendence left to this class becomes the expansion of its nationalism into globalism, the creation of a strong but struggling world-state somehow managing through hierarchy still to stand in front of the global class struggle which exists underneath it in order to prevent us, the working class, from seeing ourselves as oppressed by that instead.

Because it would remove the illusory division of nations which acts as a smokescreen for the all-too-real international division of classes, globalism would be a tremendous gamble for the bour-geoisie. But it is a gamble which the rich are increasingly being forced to contemplate due to the expansion of their world market since the end of the cold war, the increasingly severe crises this has caused their monopoly system and the threatening enormity of the working class that their newly global industry is now raising up against them.

Capitalist globalisation after 1989

Despite bourgeois nationalist ideology, the bourgeoisie continues to centralise humanity internationally at an economic level as it has strived to do since the trade fairs of the middle ages.

Capitalism abhors containment and restriction. If the nation state were genuinely to exist as an entity capable of hemming in capitalism's internationalist dynamic, capitalism would ruthlessly smash it to pieces. The whole development of capitalist accumulation has seen the knocking down of walls raised against it. The effects of free trade sent medieval city walls crashing to the ground and the hallowed walls of the guild workshops within them were then sundered like over-ripe fruit.

Such is the awesome tsunami of international capitalist surplus that it can vanquish any restrictive wall constructed against it merely by positing itself next to it. In 1989 it was at last so gargantuan that the system of exchange controls symbolised by the Berlin Wall – a wall built to protect a currency area – literally turned to dust under the dawn of television lighting.

The fall of the Berlin Wall, which forced the Soviet authorities to abandon their Canute-like attempt at holding back the torrential power of surplus value, echoed the original fall of the walls of fortified towns at the end of the feudal age. The Soviet wall crumbled for precisely the same reasons, the power of international trade raised against their system and the over-ripening of their internal economies.

They had contributed to their system's own negation by storing abroad the profits wrung from their workers since the 1950s in the form of a poltergeist currency – the eurodollar – which came battering down their doors in 1989. With the ending of the cold war and the unification of the world's bosses, a profound global economic crisis has been made possible as their world-wide pyramid scheme peaks.

World bourgeois revolution

The aftermath of future global slumps will witness the united bourgeoisie raising up to world level the state control of the economy which they ushered in as an emergency measure amongst individual nations after the Wall Street crash of 1929. This would be the horror of a world bourgeois revolution.

As in the 1930s, the aim would be the replanning of the world economy in order to ruin the remaining middle classes and peasants; only this time in order to hand over the entire planet in one go to a monopoly capitalist cartel which is now ready to act on this scale rather than on a nation-by-nation basis.

The period after 1930 is the economic graveyard of the previously national 'middle classes'. Petty-bourgeois figures such as the shopkeeper, small farmer and minor professional found that their assets and social positions were awarded upwards to the agglomerating owners of the new supermarkets, property companies and finance corporations which arose through the benevolent assistance of state planning.

The world is primed for another round of state-coordinated polarisation. Peasants now represent around forty-five per cent of the world's population; the urban working class stands at about the same level with the middle classes amounting to less than ten per cent. This compares to the figures of fifty per cent for workers, thirty per cent for peasants and twenty per cent for the middle classes which prevailed at the time of the last pilot revolution on behalf of monopoly capitalism, Hitler's ascendancy in Germany.

And so a worldwide economic slump would globalise previously national drives to 'modernise' peasantry into the cities and the crusade to crush any proletarian unrest which a world bourgeois revolution might trigger. To further deflect the wrath of a revolutionary workers' movement, while ensuring that a united planet could, despite being globalised, still appear to be somehow 'struggling' in a nationalist manner, the bourgeoisie are already globalising their Treitschkean myth of a 'World Jewish Conspiracy'. Standing in for the aristocracies, which the bourgeoisie have already triumphed over and absorbed in most economic areas, this anti-semitic fantasy is used to rally workers behind our 'struggling' bosses in their pseudo-battle with a non-existent 'Jewish ruling class'.

Leading nations have increasingly fallen back on this tired but tested bogey-story about a hidden race of manipulators now that the false opposition of the cold war has been lost to them. At various points in the 1990s the governments of Britain, France, Malaysia, Russia and Japan all publicly stated that their economic problems were due to the secretive machinations of a single 'Global Jew' (the Hungarian, George Soros). They have thus given resonance to the propaganda of the far right in America, Russia and Japan against the phantom existence of a 'Jewish world government' which is equated variously with the United Nations, the IMF or the World Bank.

The myth of a 'suffering planet' currently being pioneered by the environmentalist movement can also be seen as a prototype expansion of the myth of the 'suffering nation' used to justify monopolist dictatorship (a worldscale *Mittelstandsideologie* in formation).

The bourgeoisie's first global dictator (planet-manager) would after all require the rhetoric of globalist revolution rather than nationalist revolution in order to fabricate a mandate for truly reaching across the world and ruling us on behalf of the rich.

FAIRYTALES

World proletarian revolution

Although bourgeois society contents itself with endlessly replaying its warped record of Hegel glorifying Napoleon's modernising nationalism over ever-louder speakers, it is well aware of the truth that its negation is not a war between nations but a war between classes.

Revolutionary upheavals and wars where factions vie for control of a national territory, though terrible for their victims and onlookers, offer little to fear (and much to profit from) for the bourgeoisie. But the workers' uprising which requires no leadership but its own dialectic, demands nothing but total workers' power and rules through the direct democracy of workers' councils – this is genuine revolution. It heralds the class extinction of the bourgeoisie and their terror knows no bounds when confronted with it.

In 1847, at the earliest point at which the revolutionary workers' movement was able to issue its own manifesto, it immediately pointed to the fact that all the members of the bourgeoisie, no matter how bitterly divided they might be, would not hesitate to put aside their differences and unite to oppose the 'spectre' of a proletarian revolutionary movement, just as the seething tribal hatred of ancient Rome evaporated the instant a slave revolt broke out.

The proletariat announces its programme: the abolition of capitalism

The Communist Manifesto alludes to a revolutionary proletariat which, at the time of its writing, was still many decades away from becoming a substantial class even in economically advanced nations. With its 'less-than-scientific predictions concerning the imminence of proletarian revolution', the *Manifesto* has been attacked by bourgeois writers as an act of 'historical auto-suggestion'. But as we have seen, bourgeois society is nothing but a titanic act of on-going historical auto-suggestion. Just as the inheritors of Lenin and Stalin extolled the peasant hordes of Russia as the greatest (inert) working class of all time until at last they became that working class, so we, the revolutionary working class, are able practically to wish into existence a truly classless or 'communist' society.

We are, after all, the only class which can embody the consciousness of humanity itself by abolishing all classes. Against our dream is its shoddy counterfeit recited by every modern Western political economist (university lecturer, property developer or advertiser) who portrays the drudgery of urban existence as if it was already the imposed festival of leisure consumption which they expect to see arrive as super-profitable, surveillance-camera-ed reality.

Classless or 'communist' society

'Communist society' is the term for a global society under which the egalitarian and democratic principles proclaimed by the bourgeois revolution have finally been realised across the world. A reliable map of this world can already be obtained simply by reading off the broken promises of excitement, participation, leisure, freedom and abundance made to us every day by our present society. Despite having become technically able to deliver on a massive scale, bourgeois society constantly reneges on these promises to us because if it honoured them for more than a handful of socially isolated billionaires it would unravel totally.

Classless society cannot come about through any redistribution of wealth within our present form of society but only through the abolition of wealth in its current privatised form. Like the splinters of a broken hologram, the entire image of class society is reflected in, and can be projected back out of, any commodity which still exists as a commodity.

The redistribution of commodities merely creates the conditions for a more profitable capitalism to develop. Howard Hughes once observed that were he to commission the building of a city with free housing, hospitals and schools and then give it away for nothing to its inhabitants, he could still double his investment within five years simply by retaining ownership of one square mile of its downtown.

Classless or communist society therefore arrives with the abolition of all forms of private property and the commodity. This occurs when the human race achieves consciousness, when the world's working classes finally recognise ourselves as a united revolutionary proletariat and abolish class society.

Under the communist mode of production all forms of hierarchy throughout all social organisations are abolished through the global transcendence of the struggle between the bourgeoisie and the working class. The working class abolishes the bourgeoisie by absorbing its members just as the bourgeoisie absorbed the aristocracy during their revolution.

The proletariat becomes the final class in history and so there are no longer any classes at all. At our moment of revolutionary victory we, as the proletariat, immediately disappear. We recognise ourselves instead as the human race, fully conscious at last of being a single productive species. This point marks the end of the prehistoric phase of human development; our forty-thousand-year struggle to unite ourselves across our planet has been completed. Our breathtakingly creative adventure as nature's only conscious species can finally begin.

Work in classless society

When we, the workers, abolish private property (concepts of ownership, control and exclusion), which includes the ownership and control of all political organisations, we remove class society and the class-directed compulsion for us to work or shop.

This does not mean that human activity slows down or comes to an end. Bourgeois critics maintain that without capitalist compulsion the human race would never challenge itself to achieve as much as it does at present. This is drivel. It is precisely the limited democratic concessions and organic cooperation of the capitalist system which have been responsible for unleashing its disproportionately gargantuan productive power. Far from driving it forward, the hierarchy of class society is currently all that is left to hold those capabilities in check.

In communist society the enormous danger would come not from laziness but from people having to be dragged off their communication equipment and forced to sleep, so fanatic will be the desire to keep participating in a production process that truly belongs to us all. Just witness the insomniac dedication of computer-game players and early internet users when given access to creativity machines of the most primitive type imaginable.

International rockstars work an average of 6 to 12 hours each week.
Most of their labourtime is experienced as unbridled creativity and
they expect critical acclaim for their most facile achievements.
Their "work" even includes adulation by fans.
The few industrial diseases which affect them are derived entirely
from the pathological inflammation of the ego.
Although their talents do not exist without advanced computer
software and technicians they are the highest-paid workers in the
capitalist system, in fact they do not regard themselves as workers
at all but as "artists"

☆☆☆These are the normal working
conditions under communism ☆☆☆

Work and human creativity will have become simultaneous and thus the workaholic behaviour restricted at present to the bourgeois businessmen, who alone can hope to benefit from their efforts at the expense of the workers, will broaden out to become the playaholic behaviour of the whole human race.

Classless society is therefore the society of global mass consciousness because its driving force is the future happiness of our entire species, representing a vast expansion of bourgeois society's narrow priorities for world economic growth (the future happiness of the rich).

In a classless society we all become Hegel's 'world souls', not the fake apparitions of contemporary 'famous for fifteen minutes' superstars, but a collective race of superstars, the 'world-famous human race', a 'world species' concentrated on its future and reaching out across the entire world and ruling it together. This is total democracy.

As work in such a communist society is no longer determined by the division of labour or by access to wealth, but by democracy, it is the collective achievement of humanity acting together and not a series of selfish pseudo-achievements organised for us by a clique of glamorised bourgeois businessmen.

In our current bourgeois society their goals are allocated hierarchically to each of us, as their employees, through the factory system. Our life opportunities are limited to a set of choices over work imposed upon us by their 'labour market'. This reduction by the rich of humanity's potential to a set of limited economic options and priorities is crudely carried out in accordance with how well we have demonstrated we can obey their instructions (through our school and work records) rather than how imaginatively we can work together.

Thus is produced the appalling poverty of a world where the jobs we have had to choose determine who we are as individuals, rather than our individual dreams determining the content of our work.

This becomes clearer when we compare it to how our work might appear in a classless society. Most prominently our surplus labour (the vast proportion of our daily work) ceases to be creamed off by the rich and thus becomes available to be used as the raw material for a world of artistic creations. Sciences too advance in leaps and bounds once they escape from the restricting clutches of a few blinkered and business-sponsored bourgeois academics to become part of our general enquiry into human existence.

As the workers' movement anticipated a century and a half ago:

> … in communist society, where nobody has one exclusive sphere of activity but each can be accomplished in any branch they wish, society regulates the general production and thus makes it possible for me to do one thing today and another tomorrow just as I have a mind without me ever becoming exclusively [identified as that type of worker].[47]

Cybernetic homogenisation of software instructions and robotisation have already made this apparent Utopianism possible. For each of us could already log on to an on-going world production process whose purposes and direction we had collectively debated and decided on. We could participate in any field of this activity as simply as changing a CD in a computer-game console.

So-called 'computer hackers' have speculated on the possibilities of total democratic production by showing that the world's economy is already so integrated that from the comfort of their teenage bedrooms they could, given the right passwords, do anything from repositioning orbiting satellites to issuing the instructions to halt production in Korea's car plants.

Thus the 'night-class fatigue' which it is argued (by Leninists

47 Karl Marx and Frederick Engels, *The German Ideology*, 1845.

and bourgeois critics) would be inherent to post-revolutionary
workers' councils, where an initial euphoric rush by the masses
would be followed by a steady dropping away of active support
until the councils became unrepresentative and dominated by self-
selecting neo-leaders, is a nonsense. When workers' councils come
to embody total power then work, leisure, social life, curiosity and
participation will merge into a single, continuous creative process
throughout our waking lives. Just as capitalism seeks to fill our
every waking moment with alienation, the compulsion either to
work or shop to guarantee profits, classless society fills our every
waking moment with our own consciousness in power.

The dropping away of workers' council membership results from
fear as they are crushed by the bourgeoisie re-establishing hierarchy, never from complacency or the 'need' to return to (bourgeois)
work! The crises of communist society will not arise from apathy
but from anxiety.

Communist crises

As the workings of society become clearest when it is in crisis, so it
is best to describe the future crises of classless society in order to
illustrate the workings of a communist world. Societies are only
able to interpret crises in terms of their own levels of social development. Thus the economic crises which occurred in feudal times
– food shortages, wage inflation, unequal distribution of goods and
labour, etc. – were not understood as being economic at all. Social
control of the economy is a revolutionary bourgeois concept that
did not exist under feudalism. Problems of wealth and poverty
were understood solely in terms of religious crisis, food shortages
and crop failures were a result of 'God's wrath', not of a crude farming system which determined that the size of plots had to reflect
social standing instead of the requirements of productivity.

It took the bourgeois revolution to show that taxation and budgeting determined levels of wealth and poverty, not God's preordained social order, and that science and collectivisation could be applied to farming to make it more efficient.

Just as the future economic crises of bourgeois society existed in crude and misunderstood forms in feudal times, so the future crises of communist society also exist crudely in our world today.

As communism is the society of mass consciousness so its crises will be crises of consciousness. They may take the form of generalised doubt that we as a species are temporarily unable to achieve the goals we have set ourselves, perhaps for curing a disease or rescuing a population from environmental disaster or colonising other planets, or perhaps a more profound metaphysical crisis about our forward historical direction.

Forerunners of these future consciousness crises exist today in our bourgeois world. But they are restricted to primitive losses of confidence in the future prospects for growth of the economy rather than of human potential. Thus they can only be understood as stock-market crashes, recessions, 'downturns in the world economy', etc. Signs that we, the working class, will revolt against the increasing wealth of the rich are made to appear as if they are quasi-natural disasters affecting everybody equally.

Hints of future metaphysical crises can be detected in the enormous fascination among the general population in cosmological sciences such as quantum and chaos theories which reveal our limits in understanding reality itself (although these theories currently reveal only the limited imaginations of the conservative professors allowed the exclusive right to explore them).

The crucial crises of communist society will centre upon social doubts over our ability as a species to wish our futures into the present quickly enough for us to direct our world and history effectively. This will represent the democratisation of this tendency under capitalism where the mass coordination of consciousness appears in its alienated form, as the centralisation of capital.

The centralisation of capital

It is possible for communist society to be the society of practical dreams 'wished' into the present by a united human race because capitalists currently proceed by the same method. They wish their private futures into the present through the trading of certificates which guarantee that their present enjoyment will be paid for by the intensity of our future exploitation.

Here is the pyramid-building mechanism of capitalism; a coiled spring wrapped around our necks which enables the would-be ultra-rich to ratchet themselves into the elite off our exhausted bodies. It is known in political economy as the 'centralisation of capital'. Through this process the chief forms taken by capitalist property – real estate and machinery – are purified into financial instruments. Real estate and company equipment are used as collateral by firms as they borrow money to expand.

The individual valuations of these properties are then bundled together with thousands of others by the global financial corporations (owned by the global bourgeoisie) who can afford to lend out money cheaply, and their individual characteristics are subsumed within a single financial commodity, the bond.

In this way company shareholders who are not also bond-owners (the global middle classes) pawn the ownership of their firms by concentrating them in the hands of a few global banks and finance houses. They buy their futures from them to enjoy in the present in the form of commercial debt. If they wish to retain their ownership they must ensure that they redeem these futures through intense exploitation of the workers. This is because the values attributed to real estate, buildings and equipment against which most bonds are secured reflect the fantasy of the rich that it is their property which earns them their profits and not the workers they employ. Property prices are only the shadow of alienated labour time.

The growth of a global bond market is thus creating a correlation between the expected levels of future exploitation and our ability to resist this exploitation. The barometric rise and fall of the bond market can increasingly be read off as an efficient index of the strength of alienation and the attack upon it by rising revolutionary proletarian consciousness across the world which could eventually come to embody communist society.

Towards a global Paris Commune

Unlike bourgeois society, which endlessly predicts (and attempts to bring forward against us) an imminent paradise for itself (a playground for the wealthy masquerading as a 'leisure society' for all), the workers' movement makes no predictions. We repeatedly posit instead the arrival of our own revolutionary consciousness as the only practical means of abolishing alienation.

The revolutionary proletariat painted so powerfully in *The Communist Manifesto* finally became a reality on the streets of Paris in 1871. The Paris Commune saw the workers seize revolutionary power and form the first ever 'workers' council'. Paris became a revolutionary city in which all classes were abolished. At that point Hegel's edifice spun around on its pedestal to face us. The fact that a single workers' council has come into being has started the negation of bourgeois society and has created the possibility of our total freedom.

Since those eight weeks in 1871 the revolutionary workers' movement has moved forward, each time gleaning a more coherent analysis of our situation from the carnage of our defeats. Workers' uprisings grew in number during the twentieth century. Spontaneous though short-lived revolutions by workers (occasionally joined by genuinely mutinying students) have explored the possibilities of a classless society a little further each time before being dissipated by the preponderance of a still-dominant peasant class on the one hand, and being ruthlessly crushed by the brutality of a still-ascendant bourgeois class on the other.

The revolutionary aim of the peasantry is to dispossess their landlords and seize ownership of the land. This aim halts social revolution in its tracks as it fails to abolish class society and allows for the continued development of the bourgeoisie (that is, it moves society towards a full bourgeois revolution).

This is why the nascent bourgeoisie is swift to adopt the 'revolutionary' slogan of 'land for all' (i.e. property for all) and appeal over the heads of the minority urban working class to the peasant masses in the countryside during revolutions.

In the wake of each and every revolution carried out in peasant-based societies the bourgeoisie has proceeded to rout the working class and dispossess the peasants (in whose name it declared the revolution) through the agglomeration of farms in state collectivisation. But each time the scale of the revolution has been greater, the success of bourgeois reaction against it has been less emphatic, and the areas of the economy revealed (through their revolutionary occupation by workers) to have become proletarianised have been more extensive.

The key argument against the revolutionary workers' movement has been its defeats. Bourgeois specialists from academic radicals to Leninists have, of course, all argued that a revolutionary party is required early in a revolution to replace the spontaneous proliferations of workers' councils which, they maintain, are unable on their own to link up and abolish capitalism.

Of course the real role of a 'revolutionary party leadership' is to carry out the revolutionary agenda of the bourgeoisie – to crush workers' power and impose upon the workers' movement, and thus on society, the discipline of the factory system. It is not to assist in the linking up of workers' councils as these would then carry out the revolutionary agenda of the working class which is the abolition of all classes beginning with the services of 'revolutionary leaders'.

The power of the revolutionary working class is immense. It is as immense as is that of its own negation, revolutionary capitalism. Because of this, Leninists have only ever succeeded in crushing workers' revolution where they have been able to employ against it the primitive conditions of peasant-dominated societies. But the inevitable result of a primitive bourgeoisie such as Leninists leading a revolutionary society still dominated by peasants is the abolition of the peasantry through its transformation into an industrial proletariat.

The mission of a revolutionary peasantry is the abolition of all landlords. But such is the intensified alienation of the proletariat that our revolutionary mission can be nothing less than the abolition of all classes and their replacement with total democracy. No future Lenin, Trotsky or Stalin can hope to govern a society dominated by a revolutionary working class. This form of society governs itself through the power of workers' councils who escalate total democracy up from the earliest level of freedom, the revolutionary classless workplace, on towards the classless city, the classless society and eventually the classless species itself.

The united power of workers' councils is the unalienated form of social organisation. It appears in alienated form in bourgeois society as the capitalist boardroom meeting and, more primitively, as the executive committees of 'Communist' parties.

Rascally old pyramid schemer Dr. Sali Berisha of Albania tries to con us into "investing" in his new dot-com business down an alleyway in Philadelphia

Growing negation: Albanian revolution 1997

The centripetal logic driving the remaining backward areas of the world into the waiting arms of the advanced economies renders these leading economies increasingly vulnerable to negation.

On the day the North American Free Trade Agreement (NAFTA) came into force (1 January 1994), uniting Canada, America and Mexico in a notional customs union, an obscure guerrilla group, the Zapatistas, declared a revolution in the impoverished Chiapas region of southern Mexico. Such a declaration would have had little impact but the centralising effect of NAFTA plugged the uprising directly into the American bond markets and from there into the boardrooms of the world. Overnight 'leverage' had become a tool which could be surgically applied by the impoverished people of the world against the world's bosses.

Likewise, the grooming by Western states of the basket-case economy of Albania as a possible new member of another vast customs union, the European Union, meant that an uprising there in 1997 quickly spread consternation amongst its neighbours. A similar revolt only six years before had remained an internal affair.

Though it took place in a woefully backward economy, the Albanian revolution of 1997 took on added significance as its EU membership application was shredded in the streets. It is worth noting that all the elements of a proletarian revolution appeared during the insurrection.

Workers' councils, democratically controlled and spontaneously formed, swept away in days the repressive apparatus of a state armed by decades of Stalinism and years of Western, CIA-backed military training. The police and army mutinied on one of the greatest scales yet witnessed during a revolution. And Albania's workers' councils tossed every Leninist into the dustbin of history by successfully linking up across a whole country and seizing oil-fields, state infrastructure and the military as well as launching the first genuinely free-access revolutionary television programming. All this was achieved without any need of a guiding 'revolutionary party leadership'. At one glorious point what remained of state radio broadcast an apology to the Albanian people for imposing a capitalist economy on them while former generals were seen operating in their new, democratic capacity as advisory technicians to the committees of workers' councils.

Proletarian uprisings call the bluff of the bourgeoisie's confidence that they can wring surplus value out of us forever. And as a consequence world bond (and currency) markets fell even more heavily after Albania than they had after the Chiapas upset. It required the intervention of ten Western nation's armies to suppress the Albanian revolution. Even then mutinies by the incoming troops were reported. The international task-force hurriedly sent by Western governments to crush the Albanian revolution exposed as a hoax every illusory nationalist division. America, Germany, Britain, Greece and Turkey (these last two supposedly on the brink of war over Cyprus), France, Spain, Romania, Austria, Denmark and Slovenia, these were the nations which dropped their differences overnight and, incredibly, enlisted their forces in the Italian army to invade Albania.

This taskforce was gathered so rapidly that there wasn't even time for it to disguise its purpose with an 'humanitarian' name. It was termed the 'Multinational Protection Force'. The force assembled to protect capitalism in Albania (and bourgeois society in general) from the ultimate critique of proletarian revolution.

The uniting of the capitalists from East and West in the MPF recall the opening words of the first proletarian manifesto:

> ... a spectre is haunting Europe – the spectre of Communism. All the Powers of old Europe have entered into a holy alliance to exorcise this spectre ...

It is as true today as it was in the 1840s that all the illusory differences of nations evaporate when confronted by the real negation of proletarian revolution on no matter how small a scale.

The fresh possibility of revolution in the advanced economies

Revolutions such as those of the Chiapas and Albania are blazing signposts pointing towards America. In their wake the possibility of a proletarian revolution in the USA is stronger than ever before. The cataclysmic effect such an uprising in the original revolutionary state would have on the world is almost impossible to conceive.

It is to the detriment of all who are not anticipating the approaching insurrectionary response to America's economic polarisation and cybernetic revolution. The American population is daily growing more restless with its intensified proletarianisation (or 'downsizing') at the hands of a rampant monopoly capitalist bourgeoisie. The mass media's focus on the supposedly fascist response of the American working class to its intensified alienation in the 1990s, the proliferation of right-wing militia groups, has been employed to hide the rising tide of genuine worker unrest there, exemplified by the UPS national strike in 1997.

It may be that, just as the reassembling German government encouraged 'Freicorps' militia groups to form after World War One so that they could attack militant workers, so American militias are now being passively encouraged by the government for the showdown with America's revolutionary workers that it knows is approaching. Even if this is so there is evidence that the strategy is failing; some of the militias may end up helping to arm revolutionary workers rather than firing on them. Equally encouraging is the fact that the revolutionary situation in America's urban ghettos has extended beyond the level of ethnic unrest witnessed in the 1960s.

The workers' movement of the 1960s maintained that America's urban riots were not race riots but the first tentative uprisings against the commodity society, the most savage effects of which were then being experienced chiefly by black people. It was argued that in time this uprising would spread to all of America's ethnic groups. This has been verified – in 1992 the Los Angeles riots spread rapidly across the country and involved as many white people as black. Their targets were the shopping districts and factories of all capitalists regardless of race.

American revolution: 21st century

Few people have stopped to contemplate the power that American revolutionary workers' councils would command. Working-class Los Angelenos commented that the video of police beating Rodney King (which triggered the 1992 LA riots) was 'the first real movie to ever come out of Hollywood', presaging the awesome output and global power of a Hollywood in the hands of revolutionary workers' councils.

The workers' council itself, the form taken by revolutionary proletarians throughout the twentieth century, may even be about to be superseded. The alienated form of the workers' council in bourgeois society is the board meeting. Though few have been present at a board meeting, its image is known to us all as it is one of the most publicised of all capitalist icons. The structure of the board meeting, or 'bosses' council', has begun to alter due to the introduction of high technology, such as video conferencing and the Internet, and this may prefigure radical new possibilities for revolutionary workers.

It may be that these ponderous changes to boardroom life (presented of course by the bourgeois media as 'revolutionising business' but in fact only being adopted painfully slowly) indicate that

a genuine revolution is taking place in the potential of the workers' council, the boardroom being a cold-blooded imitation of the
real thing.

   Perhaps the workers' councils of the future will link up across
their countries and then across the globe by seizing hold of the
'information superhighway'. It will be their genius, and almost
immediately thereafter that of ourselves, which will finally allow
Hegel to sleep in his grave. At last we will be able to begin the endless adventure of class-free history.

LET'S BUILD A ROCKET

... the only purpose of a revolutionary organisation is the abolition of all existing classes in a way that does not bring about a new division of society. [It] works towards the international realisation of the absolute power of workers' councils, as prefigured in the experience of proletarian revolutions this century ... It therefore aims not at the proletarian self-management of the existing world, but at the world's uninterrupted transformation. It embodies the radical critique of political economy, the supersession of the commodity and of wage labour ... Such an organisation explicitly aims to dissolve itself as a separate organisation at its moment of victory.
Minimum Definition of Revolutionary Organisations. *Situationist International*, 1966

Towards a revolutionary organisation

The form taken by a revolutionary workers' movement has been prefigured in the revolutionary uprisings of the twentieth century. On each occasion the proletariat has spontaneously risen in towns and cities and seized its places of work and public buildings. Wherever the security services have been defeated, emergency committees and open forums have formed, based on the total democracy of daily, recallable delegates answerable to the popular decision-making process of open assemblies.

Once these committees and forums are established in more-or-less permanent session, the lower echelons of the security services and factory management then mutiny to join the workers as new members of the revolutionary proletariat.

This then is the spontaneous formation of workers' councils which together take control of society and co-ordinate a revolutionary occupation movement and the distribution of food and supplies to the people.

The democratic revolt against feudalism, which has hitherto been stalled at the level of the partial democracy of bourgeois society, now begins to move forward once more. The advent of history beckons, for, as we have seen with Hegel, feudal and capitalist societies are essentially prehistoric, having as their consciousness only the partial history of elements of the human race rather than all of it.

Private property, which necessarily encompasses state property as well (factories, hotels and government buildings), is confiscated on a massive scale by the workers who offer no compensation to the former bourgeois owners. The proletariat now see ourselves as having permanent free use of the entire social environment due to the payments we have been forced to make to create it. These are paid to the bourgeoisie by all of us through the extraction of our surplus labour under capitalism.

Unlike the emergency bourgeois act of nationalisation, this non-compensating confiscation process demonstrates the utter repudiation of private property ownership which is the first act of a revolutionary working class. Because both private and state property (factories, offices and streets) are illegally (under the bourgeois legal system) commandeered by workers' councils, the successful functioning of these councils is termed by political economists 'the dictatorship of the proletariat'.

The dictatorship of the proletariat

Under its dictatorship the working class takes on emergency powers and collectively suspends the most cherished civil right of the bourgeoisie, the right to own property. The most valuable property owned by the bourgeoisie is the surplus labour of the workers and it is therefore with the seizure of our own lives, neighbourhoods and workplaces that we start our proletarian dictatorship.

We immediately convene open forums to decide how to use the technology of capitalist society to pursue happiness. These forums are the workers' councils.

Workers' councils

A workers' council is formed from all the revolutionary members of society seizing control of that society's economy at local level, from which point they endeavour to link together in order to usurp state power and abolish capitalism. As soon as workers' councils have proliferated beyond a certain point workers immediately and consciously announce that their historic task is to abolish capitalism.

The 'workers' of workers' councils include all the people, not just those with jobs, because unemployment is a key element of capitalist economics.

The appearance of workers' councils during proletarian revolutions is not a once-and-for-all given but a developing feature of proletarian revolt. Workers' councils have no more sprung fully formed into society than has any other form of social organisation. Those who decry the failure of proletarian revolutions have failed

to analyse the advances we the working class made in forming our
own proletarian (open and non-hierarchical) organisations during
the twentieth century. The workers' councils formed in the 1905
Russia revolution were weakened by the fact that they had the tacit
co-operation of some of the liberal factory owners. Though more
advanced in their attacks on capitalism, the councils of the councilist uprisings in the 1920s and 1930s remained partially tied in
allegiance to elements of communist and anarchist trades-union
leaderships. They tended not to extend further than the specific
workforces and village populations seizing their workplaces, thus
failing to fully break free from syndicalism.

The workers' councils in the post-war Hungarian and French
revolutions marked enormous breakthroughs, with whole sectors
linking spontaneously for the first time and no separation appearing between local workforces and the general population; but they
remained held back by the ideology of nationalism (itself an indication that the ambitions of proletarian revolution had at last
reached national proportions).

In the Albanian revolution of 1997, more revolutionary land-
marks appeared with councils linking up between economic sectors and coordinating the economy, with less separation between
workers, populations and mutinying state agents than at any previous time, and with the tentative beginnings of the abolition of
national borders.

In this way our workers' councils are evolving and this is the path
that humanity must tread in order to evolve towards its own consciousness. Each time we are defeated we come closer to negating
capitalism than ever before.

Catalysts

The catalyst for proletarian uprising is never merely economic hardship, unemployment or recession; it is exasperation with the alienation of everyday life.

Lack of democratic control is the most profound reason for all revolutionary activity. Revolutionary proletarian consciousness begins to develop when we extend our sense of democratic deficit beyond the confines of bourgeois democracy, when we begin to demand direct democratic control of our lives at work and over the content and purpose of our labour.

Bourgeois capitalist society will not therefore end as a result of an enormous economic crisis (which could do no more than usher in a global bourgeois revolution). It will only experience revolutionary overthrow when it is confronted with a crisis from future society, a crisis of democratic consciousness.

Feudalism did not fall due to some overwhelming dynastic doubt about royal succession (a feudal crisis) but when it was presented with a national budget in deficit (a bourgeois crisis). This was a crisis from beyond feudal society which immediately destroyed it.

It is therefore the critical arrival of rising proletarian consciousness that will dismantle bourgeois capitalist society on first contact. The limits of our proletarian consciousness will be the only restraint on our potential as individuals in a classless society, just as it is the hierarchical restraints of fiscal budgets that now restrict us from exploring our full individual potentials under capitalism.

Notwithstanding this fact, because it originates from a more democratic basis than feudalism, an economic crisis is an alienated ghost of rising consciousness. In precisely the same movement as that of its alienated equivalent, the stock-market crash (the spontaneous co-ordination of joint stock companies), the proletarian revolution begins with an insignificant event in one sector which undermines the general acceptance of permanent capitalist alienation among all other workers.

For instance, in 1905 a strike by Moscow printers demanding the same pay for typesetting punctuation marks as they were getting for letters proved enough of a grievance to trigger a revolutionary general strike across Russia. In 1968 the complaints of a student prevented by his university from sleeping with his girlfriend in a Paris hall of residence sparked a revolutionary uprising by tens of millions of workers in France, Italy and Mexico.

Because alienation is a general, gruelling (and of course defining) feature of proletarian life, the whole working class is on permanent stand-by for virtually any grievance with which we can suddenly identify. And, once started, the revolutionary critique of alienation mounted by workers spreads to take on an exhilarating logic of its own. This is because our routine acceptance of capitalist alienation suddenly becomes dramatically overvalued when we are forced to compare our apathy to those workers who are now abolishing it. The scales fall from our eyes and more and more of us appear to spontaneously join the revolution. Soon a wildfire of revolutionary anger takes hold in every proletarianised sector of society. This revolutionary logic floods bourgeois society with light; every hidden power structure is thrown starkly into the open and its bluff is called.

The extent to which the bourgeoisie have succeeded in proletarianising the economy is also revealed.

Just as the true underlying financial strength of a specific stock is dramatically exposed when the overall froth of market expectation evaporates from it in a crash (and strong stocks either hold their value or decline gently rather than plunging with the rest of the market), so those areas of society not yet fully proletarianised suddenly stand out from the general revolutionary movement of society, resisting the uprising or else joining it in a weaker fashion than other sectors (for instance, by forming hierarchical or exclusive councils in imitation of true open-forum workers' councils).

Spontaneity

Despite the spontaneous nature of proletarian revolutions and the seemingly irrational and utterly unpredictable catalysts which spark them, they are obviously proceeded by periods of build up. After a certain point before a proletarian uprising, the remuneration of wages for industrial labour fails to secure dedication to the factory system (a system which, apart from media propaganda and terror, has no other means of securing this dedication).

Wages become inadequate compensation for the misery of alienation and workers begin to reject the illusory value which capitalist society educates us to attribute to consumer goods, desiring instead the one genuinely valuable consumer commodity that we cannot afford to buy, our own alienated labour time, or real lives. The real lives of workers (traded as commodities in huge blocks of agglomerated wastage of human potential) are goods that can only be afforded and consumed by the bourgeois class in a bourgeois society.

Once the act of increasing wages fails to secure our loyalty to the factory system, the bourgeoisie enters a perilous period. As soon as the link between consumer goods and consumer satisfaction begins to break then the act of increasing wages starts to have an effect opposite to that which has hitherto prevailed. Higher spending power only reinforces our sense of how limited our choice of life experience is. We are bombarded with information reminding us how obsolete the consumer goods we have purchased have become and how we need urgently to replace them. In a time of growing resentment towards alienation, advertising, the constant monologue on the virtues of new goods, becomes its exact opposite in our minds, a constant lecture on the worthlessness of consumer goods.

Resentment begins to manifest itself in wanton acts of destruction towards new goods and a growing romantic desire to live without consumer goods at all. Neither of these tendencies can result in revolutionary consciousness by themselves. Indeed, some lead towards reactionary mysticism, such as that inherent in much of contemporary environmental politics. But soon workers begin to voice comments which reflect the weakening grip of our enthrallment with consumer goods and our anger at wage labour.

For instance, in 1997 several United Parcels Service middle managers earning $60,000 a year immediately joined a national strike (by 185,000 people) lead by casual, non-employee deliverers despite their own positions being some of the most secure in the firm. One described his $55 per week strike pay as being a sacrifice worth making if it threatened the power of the bosses.[48]

Practical activity

If workers form revolutionary movements spontaneously and at totally unpredictable moments in history, and, in doing so, produce immediately and without rehearsal the most revolutionary form of social organisation – the workers' council – it appears on first inspection difficult to see how a revolutionary organisation that seeks to avoid emulating Bolshevism by usurping working-class power as a revolutionary bourgeoisie (and thus laying the foundations of neo-Stalinism) should behave during non-revolutionary periods.

Surely such organisations will inevitably seek to establish themselves as larval-stage emergency bourgeoisies preparing to take possession of any future proletarian revolt as their own private property?

And if the development of revolutionary proletarian conscious-

---

48 'We're not going to take it – Strike shows bitterness that US boom is for bosses only', *Independent*, 17 August 1997.

ness is the sole aim of true revolutionary organisations then, in the event of a revolutionary situation occurring, they must surely advocate their own abolition. The answer to this conundrum is to be found in the practice of revolutionary consciousness itself.

The revolutionary organisation

The purpose of the revolutionary organisation is to counter the endless demoralisation of the working class carried out by bourgeois society in its constant eulogy to hierarchical control, and to promote the concept of the international proletariat which is the starting point of revolutionary class consciousness for ourselves.

It cannot hope to achieve this unless it opposes hierarchy within itself (raises its own members' consciousness) as its first task.

The revolutionary organisation forms itself on the principle that it is necessary to oppose capitalist alienation on a collective basis. Having formed, it proceeds to raise a critique of capitalism and to explore ways of disseminating this critique throughout society.

Revolutionary critique is vital because capitalism is predicated on practical theory. Capitalism does not proceed without first justifying itself. The theory of capitalism is planning. Accountants, architects, planners, military strategists and high-level police officials are the primary theorists of capitalism's practical activity. Behind these stand the theorists employed to defend and reiterate the ideology of private property upon which that practical activity stands: lawyers, social scientists, academics, economists, massmedia editors, broadcasters and advertisers.

At the political and philosophical level the theory of rational planning and hierarchical bourgeois revolution expounded by Hegel is the organising principle of the entire system.

The first practical activity of the revolutionary organisation is therefore the critique of capitalist theory commencing with interlocking critiques of Hegel and bourgeois political economy. This is a practical activity because the dissemination of critique immediately brings the revolutionary organisation into conflict with capitalist practice as it is confronted with the problem of finding effective methods of distributing its critique without reproducing within itself the hierarchical structure of bourgeois society.

A revolutionary group raises and disseminates a theoretical critique of capitalism only if this critique is made practical by the groups' own total democracy.

> In the revolutionary organisation's struggle with class society the weapons are nothing less than the essence of the antagonists themselves: the revolutionary organisation cannot allow the conditions of division and hierarchy that obtain in the dominant society to be reproduced within itself.[49]

Total democracy

By abandoning monologue (the ownership of theory as group property) and engaging in critical debate, the revolutionary group explores the pure democracy of open-session decision-making so as to demonstrate how this could become the social organisation of society through the international proliferation of revolutionary workers' councils. Like an endlessly deliberating jury writ across the entire face of society, and judging the future of that society on a daily basis, this total democracy expands the restricted moments of consciousness allowed under bourgeois democracy – concentrated upon election campaigns and projected upon candidates.

Instead of voters being asked to select from a range of economic choices determined by the investment strategies already decided

---

49 *The Society of the Spectacle.*

upon privately by the bourgeoisie, total democracy allows us as members of a united human race to consciously choose together the future content and direction of the whole of society.

In exploring this democratic structure on as wide a scale as possible, revolutionary groups serve the important function of assisting workers' councils when they eventually form. This is because the fully critical and open revolutionary group will express itself in the theory of workers' councils – the whole of society as a huge, open and critical revolutionary group.

Theory of the workers' movement

> Proletarian revolutions ... pitilessly scoff at the hesitations, weaknesses and inadequacies of their first efforts, seem to throw down their adversary only to see him draw new strength from the earth and rise again formidably before them, recoil again and again before the immensity of their tasks, until a situation is finally created that makes all turning back impossible.[50]

The earliest conclusion drawn by the workers' movement on its activity during non-revolutionary periods is that 'the proletariat is revolutionary or it is nothing'.

By this it is understood that unless we as proletarians challenge the bourgeois control of society we can only exist, survive as best we can, eventually to die after living pointless and desperate lives, our creativity having been restricted to the production of our children (the actual meaning of the term 'proletarian').

In the eyes of the dominant class in society we workers (and our children) are mere 'instruments of production', raw material in human form. In bourgeois economic terms, workers are as dead as

50 Karl Marx, *The Eighteenth Brumaire of Louis Bonaparte*, 1852.

a ton of cotton or steel before being 'brought to life' by being entered into the production process, except that, like grain, we have the magical ability to reproduce ourselves and thus:

> the worshipful capitalists will never want for fresh exploitable flesh and blood, and will let the dead bury their dead.[51]

The lives of non-revolutionary workers are therefore, collectively, nothing more than a 'moment' in the capitalist production process.

Capitalists value dead workers over living ones in the sense that they value the dead labour frozen into their machinery above the ever-replaceable lives of the workforce who set this machinery in motion and thus generate profits for them. In other words, they value the property they own over the creative potential of the human beings they employ to produce more property for them.

But if the lives of workers are seen by the bourgeoisie as being merely a moment in the ongoing production process, these lives are still the actual living situations experienced by each of us day by day. The workers' movement realises that, in order to reclaim our lives, we workers must refuse to value those lives as the bourgeoisie requires us to, as amounting to nothing more than exploitation (the time we spend at work and shopping for consumer goods) and see instead our potential ability to live total lives.

And if the bourgeoisie weighs the lives of the entire working class as so many dead fish to be inputted into their canning process, so we must learn to see each of our lives as a precious part of the global situation of the international working class as a whole.

By employing us and measuring us collectively as an ingredient in their global production system, the bourgeoisie are condemned forever to remind us that we are a single international working

51 Karl Marx, *Wage Labour and Capital*, 1847.

class. This is the beginning of class consciousness. In response to this they therefore promote 'false consciousness' through bullying at work. At their behest we are made to 'fall in love with our own deaths', identifying with the needs of our bosses, applauding draconian laws used against us, taking pride in our self-abasement, learning to hate ourselves and love the company we work for.

All the bourgeoisie's mass media encourage just such neurotic self-sacrifice for their capitalist interests. We can be cowed enough to end up challenging each other to work harder, longer and without pay (Stakhanovism) until we become sick. Or we can rebel.

We can start to analyse our situation, work out that our bosses are our enemies and thieves, begin to steal the company's property, sabotage production, use our time at work for ourselves, start reclaiming our lives. From this point our 'analysis of our situation' begins to spread outwards.

Through our exploitation, we workers begin to recognise and identify with each other's interests rather than with those of our bosses. We begin to appreciate that not only our boss but all bosses are enemies and thieves, in fact a class of enemies, the bourgeoisie, and that capitalism is a system planned by the bourgeoisie against us. This is the revolutionary theory of the working class.

In the prelude to revolution we increasingly develop this theory of our own situation as a whole and how to overcome it. But what catapults this theory into becoming the practical means of creating a revolutionary situation is its application to all forms of pseudo-revolutionary theory which are merely masks for elevating members of the middle classes towards bourgeois power and of protecting bourgeois society while rejuvenating it.

These privately owned forms of false revolutionary contestation are ideologies. The defeat of revolutionary ideologists, the carpet-baggers and clowns who are merely dynamic capitalists in disguise, marks the beginning of full-scale proletarian revolution.

Today's Marxists... Tomorrow's Managers

CARPETBAGGERS

The new left

Even more fortunately than just having the transformations of Stalinists in Russia and China (who have at last hatched out from their long pupation as bureaucrats to become fully-fledged bourgeoisies) to educate us, we, the West's workers, also have the example of the home-grown pseudo-revolutionaries, or 'New Left' of the 1970s, to warn us of the dangers from ideologists.

Though they have failed to become a bourgeoisie in over-all charge of society, the neo-Leninist 'Trotskyists', Maoists and anarchists of the 1970s have, during the 1980s and 1990s, revealed the consequences of false contestation within advanced industrial nations.

Their supposedly revolutionary monologues have been eagerly incorporated by capitalists within the sophisticated structure of hierarchical management. By allowing former radicals to become their managers, the capitalists have succeeded in constantly revolutionising the efficiency of their domination.

False contestation

What is left today of the former would-be owners of the 1960s revolutionary movement in the advanced economic areas, the Trotskyists, Maoists and anarchists of the 'New Left' of the 1970s (the self-confessed 'professional revolutionaries')?

Having diligently learnt the methods of manipulating political committees and infiltrating local power structures, they stand contentedly today as a generation, not of leaders, but of committed line-managers.

Only pseudo-revolutionary ideologies could have imbued the monotonous tasks of line management with the glamour to galvanise these young middle-class activists sufficiently to insinuate themselves into posts always intended for them anyway. In the process they have effortlessly transformed their schooled pseudo-revolutionary hatred of 'class enemies' into a genuine contempt for the only class enemy their employers are aware of – the working class.

Whether as housing managers or home secretaries, they have achieved what their former ideologies instructed them to obtain, managerial control of the proletariat through its domination and petty local leadership. But due to the failure of the 1960s revolutionary movement (which they sought to possess) the young ideologists of the 1970s are not the overall owners of bourgeois society today. They have had to content themselves with leasehold ownership of local workforces. The freehold of the world proletariat as a whole remains in the hands of the global bourgeoisie far above them (although it does contain one former student radical, the billionaire Richard Branson).

The cult of Kronstadt

The 1921 anti-Bolshevik uprising by the same revolutionary workers' council that had previously assisted the Bolsheviks to power remains the touchstone of faith for all new-left and Trotskyist managers. Lenin and Trotsky together ordered the crushing of Kronstadt's resurgent revolutionary workers' council which was demanding a return to total democracy. Once it had been defeated they sanctioned the round up and slaughter of more than ten thousand of its members in identical fashion to Adolph Thiers who had massacred the communards after the Paris Commune of 1871 (the Bolsheviks then insulted the memory of the Paris Commune by renaming themselves the 'Communist Party' in 1922 after its heroes when in reality they had by then proved themselves to be a 'Thierist Party').

This bitter act of betrayal by a supposedly revolutionary government – whose slogan was 'all power to the workers' councils' – is frequently used to shame modern Trotskyist managers. But of course, as 'good managers', all Trotskyists are proud of Kronstadt. For them it is a Station of the Cross in terms of learning to be a radical manager. Like the Last Supper for all radical jobsworths (dynamic managers), Trotsky's massacre at Kronstadt, undertaken in order to 'save the Russian revolution', is the parable which teaches them that it is ultimately necessary to betray one's principles (and former allies) and take the 'hard decisions' that will safeguard their petty leadership positions.

For Lenin and Trotsky, Kronstadt advertised to the world's industrialists whom they were courting that they could now be relied upon to control (and sell) the previously revolutionary workers of Russia. Russia, in other words, was again open for business under dynamic new management.

Kronstadt is the ideal for which all new left managers strive. They seek, as a rite of passage into mature managerialism, the exquisite pleasure of carrying out an act of cruelty as 'regrettable' and 'difficult' as Kronstadt supposedly was for Trotsky. Every day they take pleasure in ordering up their very own micro-Kronstadts (be they evictions, social-security terminations, sackings or the removal of children) to be used against members of the working class under their jurisdiction. This is, after all the revolutionary dedication to 'good management' that capitalism demands.

Bourgeois revolutionary middle management

Former student activists have attained partial bureaucratic control over workers within the bourgeois societies they claimed to be challenging in the 1970s. In this way they have demonstrated the radical modernism of capitalism, a system which is in danger if it ever has to tolerate resigned acceptance by its workers for very long and thus demands from every worker and manager within it nothing short of revolutionary allegiance to the mundane plethora of unrewarding daily chores it endlessly commands them to view as exciting.

To facilitate this it steals the creativity and invention inherent in every genuinely revolutionary critique of its system raised against it by its bored and miserable workers (once they have failed to overthrow it) and incorporates these into an ideology for dominating the workers through further dynamic modernisation.

Capitalism does this by revising revolutionary critiques as energetic, hierarchical structures compatible with its own form, to produce more efficient and profitable methods of production.

The installation of so many former pseudo-revolutionaries in positions of management, in the advanced nations as petty officials and in the post-Soviet nations as today's new class of large-scale owners, has educated us, the world's workers.

As the manacles of false consciousness are exposed in front of us these manacles have been dissolving. Today's pseudo-revolutionaries are seen by us as being nothing more than tomorrow's managers in larval form (good students of the system). And this disillusionment is shared by the false revolutionaries themselves.

The few radicals who are still clinging to membership of neo-Stalinist and Maoist student societies cannot even convince themselves that they are engaging in anything other than learning to perform their future office work in a 'revolutionary way' (for example, chairing and minuting meetings, rigging votes and betraying their friends). This is why they have begun to refer to every workers' revolutionary uprising which now occurs exclusively in terms of the insignificant and obviously self-serving part played by the tiny numbers of revolutionary students. No worker will allow them a dream of glamour by giving any credence to their slogans and publications.

In the next revolutionary movement workers will demand to dominate our own history and creativity at all levels:

> ... this is the demand [expressed in the acts] of all proletarian revolutions, a demand until now defeated by the specialists of power who take charge of revolutions and make them their private property.[52]

So clearly does their secret desire to seize control of us show through in the rhetoric of the neo-Leninists (Trotskyists and Maoists) that it is the diffuse pseudo-revolutionary monologue of anarchism, an ideology which pretends to reject hierarchy, which now poses the greatest threat of being used to make us unwittingly hand over our revolution to new owners.

Anarchism

Anarchism is the ideology being pioneered by the world's bour-

52 *Situationist International* 10, 1966.

geoisie in order to save itself now that it has lost the illusion of Soviet opposition to its system. The rich feel threatened that we are developing proletarian revolutionary responses both to them and to their revolutionary bourgeois bureaucrats, the Leninists, whom we now recognise to be their emergency assistants.

A new form of anarchist ideology is therefore being cultivated to incorporate these responses in an apparently self-critical movement which remains hierarchical and thus harmless to bourgeois society's owners. This ideology is dynamic enough to defeat our revolution while forming the basis for an intensified capitalist system.

Since the 1970s academics in America's elite universities have been developing a new form of control from anarchism in tandem with cybernetics. This ideology is just as powerful a threat to us as cybernetics because it is designed to disguise bourgeois power as its opposite, the critique of state control and the class system (just as the Internet is constantly presented as being decentralised and uncontrolled when in reality it is totally hierarchical and facilitates global capitalism).

This development is made possible because anarchism is unusual ideologically. It is opposed to state control and, unlike other ideologists, anarchists therefore cannot consciously appear to be aiming at becoming an emergency bourgeoisie. Instead anarchists (and their ministers) regard themselves as an elite, a constituency separate from both the working class and the bourgeoisie, but nevertheless a revolutionary one, the living embodiment of 'anarchist revolution' which they see as being fully formed due to their participation in it.

Anarchist ideology resolves its conundrum of advocating an intense political activity which is separate from the everyday struggle of the workers, but nevertheless remains opposed to seizing state power (which such activity would normally aim at), by elevating anarchist potential above the revolutionary potential of the working class itself, defining anarchism as a permanently revolutionary practice regardless of historical conditions.

On abandoning the first international revolutionary organisation of the proletariat in the nineteenth century, the anarchist ideologist Bakunin set out the anarchist manifesto at a stroke when he advocated that:

> in the midst of the popular tempest, we must be the invisible pilots guiding the Revolution, not by any kind of overt power but by the collective dictatorship of all our allies.

The revolutionary dictatorship of the proletariat, involving as it would a full-scale democratic decision-making process, with all of us entitled to a say in the future direction of society, is too devoid of certainties, and too unlikely to replicate the anarchist model of revolution correctly, for anarchists to endorse it. And so they have consistently developed the 'revolutionary dictatorship of the anarchists' as a purified fantasy model to substitute for it.

In anarchist ideology and practice proletarians must first be converted to 'anarchism' before they can become revolutionary.

Anarchism is a ready-made pseudo-revolutionary consciousness which is supposed to be superior to the working class's own class consciousness. It is prepared for workers in advance by tiny theoretical groups and obscure anarchist journals which generally reflect anarchist ideology by remaining internally undemocratic and therefore more unaccountable to the working class than mainstream bourgeois political parties!

While anarchists are unconcerned with the problem of revolutionary action in pre-revolutionary times (because they preposterously maintain that their everyday lives are revolutionary and that it is for the working class to subscribe to their beliefs), they remain utterly unable to analyse their own situation.

Thus anarchists erect a pantheon of individuals and causes separate from the proletariat's struggle and judge the struggle of the proletariat in relation to how often it subscribes to these causes.

Anarchism is no longer required to theorise itself and can retreat into its own world of beliefs riven with contradictions it is not required to resolve. For instance, many nationalists from backward economic areas have absolved themselves of their intense nationalism in anarchist eyes purely by the declaration that they are 'anarchists'.

When anarchism is required to resolve its contradictions it immediately confronts the inherent difficulties and tasks, not of an anarchist revolution, but of a proletarian one.

The Spanish revolution 1936

According to the workers' movement of the 1960s,

> in 1936 anarchism really did lead a social revolution, setting up the most advanced model of proletarian power ever realised.[53]

The Spanish trades unions of the early twentieth century began, in theory, to face the reality of life for their members under contemporary capitalism. Their reaction was to revolutionise their natural syndicalism into revolutionary syndicalism.

They no longer dreamed of a society run by trades unions but of one run by the working class via the co-ordinating mechanism of trades unions. This is anarcho-syndicalism, and it became practice during the Spanish revolution of 1936. In July 1936 the workers, staring military fascism in the face, rose immediately and seized their cities, their places of work and their trades unions.

53 *The Society of the Spectacle.*

Anarcho-syndicalism is the seizure by the revolutionary working classes of their own pre-revolutionary organisations during their general seizure of society. Unlike a proletarian revolution, in which all previous working-class organisations dissolve themselves within the total democracy of workers' councils (classless society), anarcho-syndicalism preserves the trades-union organisations of the pre-revolutionary period precisely because (unlike normal trades unions) they have been previously advocating revolution as the only solution to workers' problems.

The Spanish revolution remains important because for the first time in history the lower echelons of the urban bourgeoisie momentarily abandoned their struggle for a capitalist economy (which they had failed to gain for themselves in the aborted bourgeois revolution of 1868) and united with, rather than co-opted, the social revolution of the workers.

This presaged the gathering proletarianisation of all classes under capitalism, revealed more profoundly three decades later when tens of thousands of the pseudo-middle classes mutinied and rejoined the workers in France in 1968.

Barcelona became the epicentre of the Spanish social revolution, just as it had already become the epicentre of Spanish industry, because nearly half of Spain's working class was concentrated in and around it. The revolution petered out precisely where the population was not sufficiently proletarianised. Seventy per cent of Spain's inhabitants were peasants and many were hostile to the revolution. Even those who joined it effectively created two revolutions when they collectivised their land, a rural one and an urban one, a peasant revolution and a proletarian revolution.

The anarchists in the cities were confronted by an insurrectionary squatting movement in the countryside which they were forced to recognise. Many peasants declared themselves post-revolutionary land-owners, 'parcelling out' noble estates and church lands among themselves, at the same time as the workers were announcing in the cities that all property had been abolished.

This is precisely what occurred after the Russian revolution in 1917. The rural revolution which lead to peasants seizing their land there encouraged them to:

> turn their backs on the market and make do with the primitive products they could manufacture for themselves. During the summer and autumn of 1917 this is what many of them began to do, resuming the natural economy which their fathers and grandfathers had gradually been leaving behind, shutting themselves off from the market and refusing to provide food for anyone outside their village. All Russian governments had to face this potential isolationism of the peasant communities until Stalin broke open the village economy by brute force in 1929–30 [through state collectivisation].[54]

Although the revolutionary consciousness behind the spontaneous collectivisation of their land by the Spanish peasantry had evolved to a point high enough for them to attempt to supply the proletarian revolution in the cities with food, the disjunction between the two revolutions, coupled with the dislocation of war, eventually starved the revolutionary cities into defeat.

Had agriculture been fully capitalistic then farm workers, food processors and supermarket container drivers – all proletarians in a single operation – would, in a single action, have collectivised the entire food-manufacturing and distribution process and would have been able to efficiently feed the urban revolution of which they would all have been a part (rather than falling at the paltry hurdle of seizing land).

Thus the Spanish revolution fell to the isolation of a backward

54 Hosking, *A History of the Soviet Union*, 1990.

economy and the encircling military power of bourgeois assistance for Franco (i.e. the previous defeat of the revolutionary movement elsewhere in Europe). It was weakened from within by being a popular uprising assembled in reaction to Franco's coup with a military agenda that required the organising power of the trades unions to co-ordinate it rather than being a spontaneous proletarian uprising against capitalist society. This should not obscure the fact that Spain's small working class nevertheless managed enthusiastically to seize hold of what existed of capitalism there in the most audacious and original fashion.

The military agenda of the revolution, a civil war and social revolution conducted simultaneously, guaranteed that the internal hierarchies of the pre-revolutionary workers' organisations would be placed above critique by the urgency of the situation. These would then gradually separate the organisations from the masses and see them try to independently realise anarchist ideology in government while the workers were 'beginning to realise communist society' on the ground. For what other course can ideology take but to substitute for proletarian revolution, political separation and hierarchical control?

Thus did anarchists enter the Republican government in late 1936 as ministers for anarchism, representing the constituency of an 'anarchist revolution' and proving that this is the image of a proletarian revolution as it is falling apart.

Thus did these anarchist 'leaders' then demand that the masses dismantle their barricades and return to work during the revolutionary struggle of 1937.

They eventually found themselves appealing to the workers alongside the nervous upper echelons of Republican Spain's bourgeoisie, whose plea was 'let us finish Franco first and make revolution afterwards' so as to rally the masses to a hierarchical war effort which would postpone their social revolution for ever.

Anarchist moralism

In its idealism, to which the real struggle of the working class is never sufficiently measuring up, anarchism becomes a higher revolutionary morality to proletarian consciousness. The theorists of the revolutionary workers' movement of the 1920s recognised anarchism as a diffuse ideology and criticised its moralism:

> There is one traditional political movement with an essentially 'indirect' character – which in other words presents itself explicitly as purely 'educative', moral, cultural. This is the anarchist movement. Even [the anarchists'] so-called direct action is conceived of [by them] as 'propaganda' by example. This only further confirms the judgement that the anarchist movement is not autonomous but exists on the margin of the other political movements, 'to educate them' …[55]

In recent times anarchism has added a revolutionary dimension to global social movements such as pacifism and environmentalism (to educate them!), highlighting the capitalist causes of war and pollution. But anarchists are satisfied that their analysis of these movements is revolutionary.

In this way anarchism perpetuates its monologue of an analysis which it regards as being an already fully formed revolutionary critique without the need of a revolutionary movement. Anarchism is thus the basis for a vague counter-culture which can encompass virtually any passing fad of the young – from anti-Americanism to dance music, animal rights (the political economy of anthropomorphic wildlife films) to evangelical Christianity and urban squatting.

Where anarchist causes are not the direct descendants of parochial peasant suspicion of urban government they are fre-

55 Antonio Gramsci, *Prison Notebooks*, 1933.

quently moralistic campaigns, as anarchists regard themselves as morally superior and separate to the proletariat. This tendency is aggravated by the fact that many are now the student offspring of the rich, and subconsciously loathe the workers in any case.

Where anarchists are not merely 'nursery-slope' trainees of the global middle classes they rank among the least revolutionary members of the working class. They are politicised in such a way as to have rendered themselves unable to identify with the proletariat (in effect with their own struggle) unless the proletariat first identifies with the causes of anarchism.

At the most obtuse level anarchists report on the revolutionary activity of the global proletariat (reporting on strikes, and other forms of resistance in their publications), portraying it as the global struggle of the workers towards anarchism rather than towards proletarian revolution.

Anarchism, though weak, remains the most powerful ideology standing between the working class and its full revolutionary consciousness because anarchists stand at the entrance to revolutionary critique demanding an entrance fee from workers who are at last challenging their oppression. For this reason it is yet possible that anarchism will come to be fashioned into a diffuse ideology of hierarchical state power during a revolutionary crisis in which the working class has already driven off all forms of Leninism.

Anarchist ministers

4 November 1936 marks the point at which the dreams of the revolutionary working class of Spain, men and women who identified their life and death struggle as anarchist, were drowned in a bucket of betrayal which held fascism and defeat in its dregs. On this day anarchist ministers took their seats in the Spanish parliament and gave birth to a notion which is reaching maturity in our own time,

that, when every other method has failed, the bourgeoisie can clothe itself in anarchism to save itself.

The emergence of anarchist ministers in revolutionary Spain is a clear reminder that anarchist leaders and organisations (as opposed to the revolutionary masses) ultimately regard themselves as a separate community and constituency which stand above the revolutionary working class and can therefore participate within the power system as a sort of self-criticism of the state from within.

So Dutch and German anarchists of the 1970s and 1980s got elected to city councils supposedly in order to represent the 'squatter critique' of local government, and the academic Noam Chomsky educates America's Ivy-League student elite and lectures on network television while presenting himself as self-criticism by the university and mass-media.

It is this pseudo-critical incorporation of prominent anarchists within state power that allows bourgeois society to deflect genuine proletarian attack away from itself. Encouraging us to regard our anti-capitalist struggle as 'anarchist', it makes us identify with the collaboration of anarchist ministers who supposedly represent us.

Bourgeois society is now going beyond this stage and developing anarchism as the next means of oppression.

As anarchist ideology demands recognition for anarchists as a 'revolutionary minority', it is inevitable that their organisations should seek incorporation in government while glibly maintaining that this is not collaboration but represents instead the critique of government.

This has provided the basis for the merger of modern anarchism with 'green politics', the political environmentalism which is funded and sponsored by global financiers as a new Malthusian attack on the working class as a horde of supposed polluters.

Anarcho-environmentalism

Anarcho-environmentalism finally allows anarchists to immerse themselves in an entirely separate world of revolutionary needs against which stand both capitalists and workers who have not accepted anarchist ideology.

Anarcho-environmentalism is the full culmination of anarchist elitism, moralism and separation. It facilitates anarchists with their justification for a morally superior programme of direct action (specifically anarchist action which it is up to the rest of the working class to endorse) while validating their sudden acceptance of anarchist ministers who are now widely proliferating in the form of 'fundamentalist' green politicians.

All the outrage expressed by rank-and-file anarchists at the appearance of anarchist ministers 'representing them' in 1930s Spain (and at local level in 1970s and 1980s Holland and Germany) would seem to have peacefully dissipated. With the anarcho-environmentalist movement happily operating within the (neo-Malthusian) orthodox environmentalist movement (paid for by the super-rich) as its wise and noble conscience, the anarchists have democratised Bakunin while assisting the bourgeoisie in perfecting its new revolutionary ideology.

They have replaced the elite of revolutionary anarchist 'pilots' envisaged by Bakunin with a whole movement of pseudo-revolutionary bungee-jumpers, all of whom happily defer to a new hierarchy of green politicians, pseudo-scientists, and media stars in their meaningless struggle to 'save the planet' from its misuse by the working classes.

Today, welcoming the fact that they will increasingly find themselves ushered towards state power once more orthodox attempts to control us have been defeated, anarchists and their more openly hierarchical associates, the Trotskyists, are keen to claim ownership over our revolutionary responses to capitalism. They seek to

ECSTASY AIRPORT!

During the early 1990s the South African military manufactured thousands of kilos of low quality Ecstacy to finance a dirty-war in the townships (Project Coast).

In November 1992 they shipped a consignment to Britain, hidden in the nose-cone of a Springboks jet. South London gangs then distributed it across Britain's club-scene.

(Source: Truth and Reconciliation Commission)

PRODUCE OF MORE THAN ONE COUNTRY

MADE IN SOUTH AFRICA

drug rave-up in hangar

redefine these in advance so that our responses will accord with their monologues.

So, while Trotskyists offer us endless false praises, acknowledging our struggles as the preparation for their future rule over us, anarchists criticise us for not rebelling correctly in accordance with their already issued instructions!

Only if a revolutionary dialectic develops will we, the working class of all nations, be able to sweep aside these buzzing wasps lulling us into handing control over ourselves to them and establish instead a true, non-hierarchical democracy. Only then will the next social revolution feature us confronting our historical task unmediated by these would-be managers waving red or black flags with party names stitched carefully across them in advance (and with bourgeois bribes in their pockets). Only then will we be able to prevent our world proletarian revolution from being stolen from us and turned into its hideous counterfeit – a world bourgeois revolution.

Against the appearance of councilist ideology

If anarchism, which does not seek state power, can nevertheless become an ideology, capable of separating working-class anarchists from their own struggle as proletarians, how can the theory of proletarian revolution through the formation of workers' councils itself avoid becoming an ideology?

Firstly, the spontaneous formation of workers' councils was the actual practice of proletarian revolutions during the twentieth century. No revolutionary group nor revolutionary ideology has been able to ignore this fact and nor have the established bourgeoisies which have been swift to dispatch their mercenaries at the first sign of a proletarian revolution in order to assist even ostensibly 'revolutionary' governments in their suppression of it. Time and again the bitterest of enemy nations have suddenly assembled their warships together in the harbours of any region where the working class has temporarily seized power.

The ideologists of revolution are those who set out to subvert the total democracy of the rank-and-file workers' councils and establish a leadership to guide, unite or control them.

The most immediate method for a revolutionary group to avoid developing within itself an ideology of workers' councils is for its members to acknowledge that their status as proletarians compels them to recognise the revolutionary movement which they are advocating as being the only means to their own liberation.

There is no separation between their goals and those of the rest of the working class; their pre-revolutionary research is part of the faltering progress of proletarian research; the desperate need for an end to alienation is as urgent for them as for all other proletarians.

Maintaining wonder at the possibilities of a proletarian revolution and an urgent desire for the marvellous adventure it would make possible are the prerequisites for any genuinely revolutionary movement.

Boundless optimism is justified by the everyday phenomenon of capitalist technology which requires only democratic control to realise itself as an incredible world of endless creation.

We actually do live in a society which can move vehicles around on the surface of Mars. Who then can regard the possibilities of proletarian revolution as Utopian?

Our creativity is endlessly wasted because so many of us have had our self-confidence and imaginations crushed, twisted and suppressed for so long, bombarded by a world shaped for us by the meanest intelligences, lowest-common-denominator planners and the most cynical designers.

Situationism (the last form of ideology)

Councilist ideology is the final desperate weapon that a revolutionary bourgeoisie can seize upon in order to prevent our proletarian revolution from obstructing their control. It would require the sacrifice of most of the prevailing members of the bourgeois class because the triumph of this ideology would denote the overthrow of virtually all existing bourgeois owners (and their notions of private property) by a new, global revolutionary bourgeoisie claiming to act as the collective will of the revolutionary workers.

The private property created by this new bourgeoisie would be nothing less than a claim of ownership over the creative potential of the entire human race. This it would render, 'on our behalf', into the intellectual property of some hideous, pseudo-democratic global state. Eventually, of course, this global-state-owned creativity would be privatised and handed out to an international monopoly leisure industry of the future.

Already hinted at in the twisted slogans of post-Trotskyism and neo-anarchism, this ideology exists at present only at the 'trilobite' stage of its evolution, termed at present 'situationism' after the most recent theorists of councilist uprising. But it was these very theorists who warned us that such an ideology could appear.

They reminded us, their inheritors, that:

> … our only path, which is obviously going to be long and difficult, has nevertheless been mapped out: the formation of councilist organisations of revolutionary workers, federating with each other on the sole basis of total democracy and total critique.
> Our first theoretical task will be to combat and refute in practice the last form of ideology the old world will set against us: councilist ideology … [some groups in their time had already] expressed a preliminary gross form of this ideology, quite simply proposing that workers' councils should be elected above the general assemblies, whose only task would

thus be to ratify the acts of this wise revolutionary neoleadership …
The next revolution will recognise as councils only sovereign rank-and-
file general assemblies in the enterprises and the neighbourhoods, whose
delegates are always subject to recall and derive their power only from
those assemblies. A councilist organisation will never defend any
other goal …[56]

Because of the vast proletarianisation of the world's population
since the 1960s, even this declaration appears primitive.

The formation of councils has already broken out of the separation between workplace and neighbourhood. So total has capitalist
practice become that its negation now begins with the seizure of
whole cities and economic sectors. Through colonisation, monopoly capitalism has integrated work, transportation, leisure, home-
life and the environment.

The councils of today would seize these spheres of operation
simultaneously. And rather than operate through the medium of
recallable delegates, the councils of the future may follow those
alienated apparitions, the capitalist boardrooms, and use Internet
links to convene global conferences. It will be our adventure as
workers to explore the possibilities of total democracy.

Islamic revolution: Iran 1978

Unlike the ideologies of Leninism currently hibernating in the
advanced economies, today's revolutionary agenda in the still-
backward economies is increasingly dominated by clerical nationalism.

Have emerging revolutionary bourgeoisies now abandoned their
tendency to turn radical political economy into dynamic national-

---

56 *Situationist International* 12, 1968.

ist ideology? Are they genuinely returning their societies to the pre-Enlightenment mysticism of absolute religion?

In 1978 Iran witnessed one of the most powerful revolutions in history. Millions marched in insurrection through the cities of the most repressive regime on earth and sounded its death knell. Workers and market traders seized the streets and factories, tens of thousands of managers and factories bosses ran for their lives and the armed forces briefly appeared to disintegrate.

To a far greater degree than in the Russian revolution of 1917, the Iranian revolution witnessed the uprising of an entire people against a despot, an army and a massive secret-police force, all of whom were swept away by an urban revolution while peasants seized land in the countryside. What has shocked revolutionaries since this event is the fact that the revolution was allegedly carried out in the name of militant Islam. Of course, a welter of academics has drawn the conclusion that this 'Islamic revolution' demonstrates that the era of workers' revolution is over and that a more diverse, postmodern concept of societal development must be hurriedly installed. Discrediting workers' struggles is after all their job.

But the Iranian revolution marked no return to religious feudalism. Iran's revolutionary bourgeoisie did not restore the absolute monarch deposed by the people but declared a bourgeois revolution, in exactly the same terms as in post-revolutionary Russia.

The revolution of the urban workers was at first co-opted by the revolutionary middle classes and then crushed in isolation when these middle classes appealed over the heads of the workers to the peasants whom they courted with the traditional lure of free petty land ownership.

The revolutionary middle classes who were seeking to become Iran's bourgeois rulers did not return the country to feudal Islamic rule but instead twisted Islam into a new, expedient form of political economy.

They did not proclaim their revolution in the name of some new variant of Marxism (such as Trotskyism or 'situationism') because they were not confronted by a large or sufficiently advanced proletariat forcing them to do so. Although they proclaimed it in the name of 'militant Islam', the main publicly stated preoccupations were not righteousness but economic planning and the preservation of private property.

The expediency of the Islamic revolutionaries has been breathtaking. They have co-opted every element of the Iranian revolution, from its mosque-based organisation under the eyes of the Shah's secret police to its spontaneous seizure of the factories and oil interests of an imperialist-backed ruling class, and absorbed them beneath the supposedly pious veil of a very earth-bound religion, an 'Islam of protected investment'.

The party of the revolutionary bourgeoisie, the Islamic Republican Party (IRP), set about breaking the workers' movement in Iran (whose highest achievement was the Iranian revolution) by closing universities and swamping factories with their counter-revolutionary 'Revolutionary Guards'.

The Iranian revolution (like the Algerian revolution of 1963) was carried out by a very isolated proletariat who nevertheless established workers' councils in whatever industries were in existence, only to see those councils crushed by a larval bourgeoisie clothing itself in religious nationalism. The revolutionary party of the clerical middle classes, the IRP, seized political power between 1979 and 1983 in identical fashion to the Bolsheviks in Russia before them, a process made possible by the persistence of a large peasant population whose revolutionary demands could be comfortably accommodated by the new regime and used as a shield under which it could crush the urban workers' movement.

While that movement was still unassailable there were early forced compromises between it and the regime. These compromises carried the seeds of its destruction within them, as an observer has noted:

> The formation of workers' councils in factories was so widespread in the early days of the new [Iranian] regime that Ayatollah Beheshti, head of the Supreme Court and powerful leader of the IRP, advised employers, 'If factories could be better organised with councils, they should be accepted … It is not possible to run a factory with bayonets'. … His notion of workers' councils differed from that of the workers, however, because he suggested that such councils be composed of workers, management, and owners of industry.[57]

These poisoned compromises were rapidly accelerated into out-and-out attack once the revolutionary bourgeoisie felt strong enough:

> … workers' councils presented a threat to the government and as such were opposed by both liberal and clerical factions of the government. Both factions of the government instead favoured private property and the right of the owners to realise profits. The new constitution also recognised the owners' right to possession and profit …
>
> As a result workers' councils came under government attack. The government charged that interference by councils in management reduced efficiency … During the summer of 1980, the [IRP-controlled Islamic police] dismantled the councils and purged large numbers of their members and activists from the factories.[58]

So much for the spiritual concerns of those members of the bourgeoisie who announce that by taking over ownership of a revolu-

57 Misagh Parsa, *Social Origins of the Iranian Revolution*, 1989.
58 ibid.

tion they are bringing the laws of heaven to bear on earth (in whatever form heaven is most familiar to their local populations). Beneath the bizarre foliage of whatever toxic regime takes root in a defeated proletarian revolution one will always find, in reality, the far-from-spiritual bourgeois preoccupations with efficient industrial production, the preservation of a climate suitable for profitable business, and a universal respect for private property.

CLOWNS

False consciousness

Capitalism is constantly attempting to do away with the role of line-managers by increasingly incorporating the functions of line-management within its machinery. This has the effect, not of abolishing line-managers, but of downgrading them as power figures, causing the senior managerial class to be increasingly replaced by a massive proliferation of low-grade office managers, auditors and accountants, a layer of workers merged increasingly closely with the industrial proletariat they are supposed to be controlling (hence the rise of employee-participation schemes where workers are encouraged to help manage themselves on behalf of the bosses).

The pseudo-middle classes can only be distinguished from the proletariat proper in terms of their enforced false consciousness.

Due to their roles in maintaining capitalist control, managers are forced to identify with the ideology of their bosses, the bourgeoisie (workers are encouraged to do this voluntarily – we are forced to obey the ideology of our bosses whether we identify with it or not). This is an ideology which, for all but the very highest-placed managers, is in total opposition to their own class interests.

For this reason, once a proletarian revolution begins in earnest, many thousands of lower and middle managers will suddenly join it. Indeed, the liberation of their consciousness indicates the high-water mark reached by the revolutionary masses as a whole and reveals the extent to which underlying proletarianisation has penetrated the management functions of the economy.

The problem of the technical pseudo-middle class for the proletariat only arises when line-managers start to become revolutionary theorists for the workers' movement. As they are generally skilled workers this is in no way unacceptable and indeed it is necessary. They help to theorise our movement by using their working experience against the bosses, bringing their knowledge of the managerial and technical requirements of the owners – budgeting, organisation, international linkage, operation of equipment, etc. (much of which they are trusted to keep secret from the workers beneath them) – over to our side to be utilised by us against the bourgeoisie.

It is only when managers fail to identify completely with the workers' movement and attempt to carry over some of the minuscule privileges and enforced respect they enjoy under the capitalist system into the workers' movement that they become a threat to us. This is when managers attempt to theorise on behalf of the workers instead of with us, when they attempt to theorise the position of the workers below them, instead of that of themselves and the bosses above them, just as when they attempt in their everyday lives to organise our workplaces on behalf of the bosses.

These manager-theorists therefore fail to abandon the bourgeois ideology they are forced to embrace. This type of manager theorist is the so-called 'professional revolutionary' or 'specialist', a revolutionary who attempts to 'manage revolution' and advance from being pseudo-middle class to becoming the real thing.

Naturally enough, this ideological position reaches its zenith not in the workplace but in the establishments set up by the middle classes to train managers – the universities.

The ultimate hierarchical manager-theorist is the theorist whose job it is to teach future managers about hierarchy in the first place (through obedience to the hierarchy of lectures and grading). This is the tenured academic, the pure model from the genuine middle classes who is employed to convince technicians that they should mimic the elitism of the real middle classes and side with their bosses against us.

Senior academics

Senior academics, as members of the world's middle classes, are among the highest ideologists of bourgeois society. They are paid to reinforce and perpetuate the pyramid conditions of class society by hierarchically grading human beings.

If these senior academics are clowns, then as ideologists they are capable of being sinister ones. They are quite prepared to grade human beings to death if required to do so.

The roving death squads sent into Poland by the Nazis to carry out the holocaust exterminations during the 1940s were not drawn from the regular German army. They were elite units recruited from the upper-middle classes and contained the highest number of doctorates in any section of the military. Academics were chosen for this sadistic and brutal work because only they could be relied upon to have sufficient 'ideological motivation'.[59]

In more normal times senior academics exclude the vast bulk of the working classes from access to their universities and in doing so ensure that the content of university courses and academic theory is pure bourgeois ideology no matter how sophisticated it appears.

59 Ham Bresheeth, Stuart Hood and Litza Jansz, *The Holocaust for Beginners*, 1994.

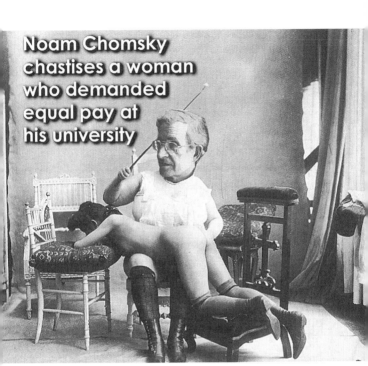

Noam Chomsky
chastises a woman
who demanded
equal pay at
his university

They then stratify their students by marking them in accordance with how well they can demonstrate an aptitude for conforming to this ideology on their own initiative.

The bureaucrats and commercial functionaries required by capitalism are thus reproduced because, at one remove as they are from the immediate conditions of the factory system, academics are free to explore the theory of line-management. After all, the academic is paid by capitalist society to theorise line-management and propagate line-managers in the form of university graduate students.

That gross enemy of the workers, the 'radical' academic, compounds this hierarchical production of line-managers with a hierarchical theory of revolution and thus produces a theory of revolutionary line-management (or dynamic capitalism).

Radical academics

Bourgeois society employs radical academics to anticipate for it the appearance of our revolutionary attacks and, where possible, to redesign these attacks as the basis of a new revolutionary bourgeoisie to use against us.

The unexpected ferocity of the Iranian and Nicaraguan revolutions which caught the American government off guard lead to that pilot nation of capitalism elevating the liberal critics of its foreign policy into prime positions in its most prestigious universities during the 1980s.

Here they were paid to explain to the up-coming student elite of America's business class how to forecast a rising tide of protest against American imperialism and from this point how to forecast the appearance of anti-capitalism among the workers of all nations.

These are today's 'anarchist' academics, arrogant self-publicists in themselves, who are of enormous assistance to the world's busi-

ness class in informing them how to head off our revolutionary
explorations.

All radical academics make sure they are comfortable in their
tenured university posts before they theorise revolution. The 'radical' professors have long had their warblings faithfully reproduced
by their vanity publishers, the Leninist and anarchist presses (the
'obscure journals' we have already encountered).

The professors' best lectures concern their own self-importance,
and they make sure that their every written idea carries their sur-
name as a registered trademark (it is they, and the pop-music
industry, who have pioneered the protection of intellectual property). They forlornly believe that we will enact their ideas (which
are merely stolen elements of our own critique in any case) with
their superimposed in our minds, like the perpetual logo in
the corner of a cable-television transmission. They offer up their
'revolutionary thoughts' for criticism in identical fashion to their
reactionary colleagues with whom they share their tea-rooms.

They will only accept, or comment on, criticism of their work by
members of the same elite, members who agree by mutual consent
to recognise these ideas as their private property.

If their students were to mutiny and challenge their control of
the lecture hall (reject their hierarchical marking system, in other
words) they would ring themselves with police in an instant.

Here then are the professor heroes of the Trotskyists and anarchists, the Chomskys, Bookchins, Alan Woods, Sadie Plants and
all other 'extreme radicals' who are nothing more than variations of
Alan Sked,[60] ludicrously dreaming of their works being carried by
their disciples to the barricades, presumably so that the workers

---

60 Alan Sked was a right-wing lecturer who carried out the erotic dream of all academics and launched his own political party (i.e. his ego raised up to the level of
   national politics), the extreme nationalist UK Independence Party.

can be enrolled there as their new forced-to-adore-them-for-good-grades students.

Radical academic monologue

The only revolutionary act which it is possible for radical academics to carry out is the revolutionary seizure of their own egos (their working environment). This act underpins all the other ostensibly revolutionary positions which they may market in their self-proposed role as the emergency intelligentsia of an emergency bourgeoisie.

Academic revolution aims at a world that can only be legitimated through prior consultation with academics. This is why so many radical academics in the 1990s effortlessly adjusted their desk-bound dream of becoming a hero-worshipped Marxist revolutionary leader (in the mould of Che Guevara) into its contemporary version, becoming a Euro-federalist leader (in the mould of Vaclav Havel).

The radical academics' vision of revolution (velvet or otherwise) remains identical of course: all of society gazing up at them in awe as if in a gigantic lecture theatre.

Few will ever realise their dream of becoming philosopher-kings though their televised 'rally' outside the World Trade Organisation in Seattle in 1999 might have proved an ideal electoral college to anoint an academic 'pope' if the fierce competition between their egos didn't make this impossible! But the massive expansion of the mass media since the 1970s has opened up the possibility for academics to achieve neo-leadership positions in society without the need to engage in political revolution.

No analysis of academics would therefore be complete without a description of the new theories of the ego which they have devised to enable them to embrace the fame-giving powers of the media while continuing to serve their employers' interests. (Rebellion against those employers is not a viable element of any radical academic agenda.)

These are the theories, the pure academic monologues, which they have dutifully developed since their old employer, the State, became supplemented on campus by the corporate sponsorship of universities after the 1960s. Collectively they have termed them 'postmodernism'.

Academics fondly imagine that their new theories have propelled them into a hallowed autonomy, have at last made them a totally independent intellectual elite. According to them the mass media have replaced reality in modern society and, as only they can interpret the mass media, they must be permanently consulted by and through them.

The need to become stars which the commercialisation of universities has visited upon them has caused academics to idolise the mass media. They have accordingly theorised the television studio as an extension of the lecture hall. By adopting postmodern theories most previously 'radical' academics have now abandoned trying to recruit the workers to their revolutionary cause (and debating whether or not they, as intellectuals, can still be classed as 'workers' themselves) and have announced instead the meaninglessness of workers' revolution.

In this way they have honoured their responsibility to serve the interests of their bosses, the owners of universities, who pay them to theorise worker defeat, and have placed themselves, theoretically, above the workers in a new way, as a priesthood of fame.

The new aim of academics is to become permanent adjuncts to the mass media, competing with each other to use them as their own 'karaoke machines' for amplifying their amateur egos.

Postmodern theories may have developed as the natural voice of academic self-importance but they are not innovative, they are derived from the original edict given to academics in the twentieth century by their employers, to investigate the structures of control (management).

Structuralism

> Structure is the daughter of present power. Structuralism is thought underwritten by the State … its method of studying the code of messages is itself nothing but the product, and the acknowledgement, of a society where communication takes the form of a cascade of hierarchical signals. (Guy Debord, 1967)

The agenda of the academic theorists of the late twentieth and early twenty-first centuries is underpinned by their instrumental inability to think beyond the instructions and environments provided for them by their employers. Far from being original, the banality of modern academic theory is breathtaking. Its source in the twentieth century was structuralism, capitalism's attempt to bring theory into line with its practice of imposing structures on workers' behaviour. At the individual level though structuralism is the merging together of the two main strands of an academic's consciousness, his own ego and the conditions of his employment contract.

The owners and sponsors of universities, States, capitalists and the military, require academics to assist in the construction of capitalist planning systems. Consequently academic social theories must succeed in reducing human behaviour as closely as possible to the structures compatible with the operation of capitalist machinery. In this way they mimic the structuralist requirements demanded by capitalists from the other academic sciences they sponsor. Therefore the ultimate dream and goal of structuralism is cybernetics, the robotisation of the workforce and the total planning of the environment against workers.

The foundation of structuralism in social theory is the study of linguistics (language structure and semiotics) artificially divorced from social practice and elevated above class struggle. In other words, the foundation of structuralism is one of the basic priorities of capitalism, to find out how workers can be made more compatible with the instruction manuals, advertising slogans and mechanised routines of bourgeois society.

Because language is dialectical and cannot be meaningfully separated from proletarian struggle against bourgeois power, the hope that the academic study of communication and language as it exists within bourgeois society could reveal any valuable insights is laughable. Genuine communication can only be achieved as the movement towards abolishing capitalism develops, being realised through the formation of revolutionary workers' councils, public forums for the seizure of bourgeois society. At this point our voices, as working-class women and men, are listened to for the first time.

Only when all humanity is able freely to discuss and decide together the future possibilities of our own lives will language have advanced to the stage of real communication. It is obvious therefore that the non-revolutionary study of communication will become the study of how to restrict communication further, how to reduce communication to one-way instructions, to the dictates of capitalist production encoded within the operating systems of its machinery and planning.

The academic study of language structure achieves this aim while simultaneously existing as a study of hierarchical knowledge.

Because the lecture notes of university professors are the form in which hierarchical knowledge is most familiar to them, they have become the subconscious basis for their theoretical analysis. Unchallengeable by students, if they wish to obtain good grades, these notes are the embryonic form taken by the unchallengeable instructions of the bureaucratic line-managers these students later encounter and become in their working lives.

Since the successful introduction of an intense and universal factory system across the advanced economic nations during and after World War 2, academics have been required by their employers to widen the scope of their structuralist analyses. Academics have been allowed by their bosses to wander from structuralism into areas of their own choosing.

So rapid has the development of cybernetics become that the bosses themselves have not been fully confident that they can anticipate the best methods of increasing its savagery against workers, and so they have requested that their middle-class employees, the academics, explore the possibilities for them.

Left momentarily to their own devices, the academics have been largely unable to develop theories any more complex than the study of their own immediate environments, their lecture theatres, their hierarchical relationship with their students and their vanity publications, such is the staggering poverty of their intellectual lives.[61]

Their advance on structuralist theory, uninspiringly termed 'post-structuralism', equates human experience exclusively with (individualistic) language structure. In other words, the features of their workplace, the lecture hall and the sound of their own voices, become for them the whole of reality.

Post-structuralism is therefore the theory of unification between academics and the mass media. So shockingly bankrupt are the syndicalist explorations of academics that they make the syndicalist dreams of trades unions seem noble by comparison.

---

61 Nevertheless corporate capitalism actually managed (briefly) to harvest a reward from these meanderings. 'Post-colonial theory' was adapted for a few years in the late 1990s by British Airways to provide the imagery it needed to escape from its national-carrier status. Its new, diversified ethnic livery announced it as one of the first major companies to embody globalised capital, 'local' to all (creditworthy) areas of the world. This finally realised the old academic joke that writing conference papers is simply 'turning bullshit into plane tickets'.

Post-structuralism

With the advent of post-structuralism the unequal struggle in the minds of academics between their egos and their employment contracts is temporarily resolved in favour of their egos.

Finally admitting to themselves that structuralism is an invention they have been required to impose on reality by their bosses, academics do not then conclude that human communication is dialectical.

Rather than confess that the idea of society's structure emanating from the non-historical structures of language is ridiculous, they follow the opposite route.

With post-structuralism, academics elevate the importance of language, which refers solely to the over-arching importance of their own voices and writings, above everything else. Unable to face the challenge of the vast potential project of proletarian revolution which would sweep them aside, their (still essentially structuralist) theory of post-structuralism substitutes reality for a diversity of signs, language games and aimlessly uncompleted 'meta-narratives'. In other words, post-structuralism is the belief by academics that their ideas are so profound that they can be substituted for reality itself!

The catch-all term used to describe the increasingly unserviceable theories of the academic milieu is the 'postmodernist project' which encompasses post-structuralism.

Postmodernism

Because the starting point for all postmodernist theories, structuralism, is naturally non-historical, the postmodernist project leads academics back to their primary task of denying the existence of history and progress, of neutralising the historical theory of Hegel when the proletariat seize hold of it (that is, when we threaten to seize hold of bourgeois society).

Structuralism is anti-historical because the structures which hold workers in place under capitalism can only ever be portrayed by it as being timeless laws. Otherwise the ultimate historical structure of capitalist society presented as being timeless, private property, would become contestable. The structural theory most antithetical to history is Marxism, which attempts to claim for late-emerging bourgeoisies the private ownership of history itself in the form of class struggle. Classes appear as timeless, almost geological phenomena, not living, struggling people.

Post-structuralism furthers the non-historical 'insight' of structuralism by denying the existence of history altogether, claiming that the concept of history is an invention of language. None of this is any theoretical advance over easily observable capitalist practice. As early as the 1920s, capitalism was demonstrating by itself how it intended language structure to replace history. American factories were then employing ex-peasants recently arrived from Europe who could be profitably made to work together despite being totally unable to speak or understand a common language. The only language they were required to understand by capitalism was the language of the automated production line. Henry Ford's car factory pioneered the teaching of language to these immigrant peasants with an on-site language school called 'The Sociology Department'.

The first lesson taught in this primitive version of the modern university was the benevolence of the factory owner Henry Ford himself (the only historical figure allowed to be theorised by Ford's 'academics'). This was followed by instructions on how to obey factory officials, how to continue obeying factory regulations in home life (or risk being sacked) and how to save enough money to buy a Ford motor car.

This then is the structure of language which capitalism requires to be made universal, a language which teaches through regulated production that history commences with the benevolence of a factory owner.

Today's 'Henry Fords' who finance the modern universities expect them to serve as contemporary sociology departments (as well as research-and-development departments on the technical side). At the social level capitalism requires only the study of semiotics, the science of signs, so that it can instruct workers more efficiently how to use its equipment without them understanding its purpose or possibilities.

Fame

Of course postmodernism can be described in total quite simply as being the most concerted effort yet assembled by academics to refute the theory of alienation on behalf of their employers. Postmodernist theory is simply the longest love-poem yet composed by academics to the global capitalists who have inherited Henry Ford's supposed benevolence.

By replacing the study of history with the study of linguistic structures academics have endeavoured to abstract from theory and from reality the concept of alienation. Reinforcing alienation is, after all, their job and the scientific study of alienation is not their task but ours as a revolutionary proletariat.

Postmodernism is, in total, an elaborate project of mean imagination designed to surgically remove the theory of alienation from the theory of Hegel, to deny, in other words, revolutionary theory of historical progress to the working class.

Due to the sterility of this project modern academic theory has swiftly reduced itself to an absurd self-congratulatory song of praise sung by academics to themselves (as the only permitted owners of critical knowledge) and to their fellow stars in the media.

Thus they 'explain' the philosophical significance of television programmes, pop records and Hollywood movies, etc. All this is nothing more profound than a third-rate 'philosophy of fame'. Or put more simply the scientific study by academics of the importance of themselves and their fellow celebrities.

Postmodernism has quite rightly rendered academics a laughing stock in the eyes of the working class but then their theories are designed to be a perpetual hosanna to the ephemeral famous elite of which they fondly believe themselves to be members.

Postmodernism is an ever-more sophisticated method by which academics can express their contempt for the only genuine scientists and theorists who threaten their exulted positions, revolutionary proletarians.

Meanwhile, capitalist society itself has happily continued, despite the academics pronouncing it postmodernised. Nevertheless, it has wisely acknowledged the academic glorification of fame. Fame is a vital mechanism of capitalist society (and its media) as its strives towards mass-producing Hegel's World Soul in a readily disposable form.

These transitory world-ghosts (images of real living people, famous for 15 minutes and more profitably famous once dead) endlessly pass in front of us as an homogenised parade of temporarily televised superstars. Indeed, fame is increasingly being proletarianised as mass low-waged employment in the service industries begins to encompass entertainment, media and leisure.

This proliferation of low-grade, non-remunerative fame is intended by capitalism to reproduce a new reactionary pseudo-middle class of workers who irrationally identify with their bosses to replace the pseudo-middle class of technicians it is rapidly losing to proletarianisation.

So, while academics have been merrily pronouncing Reason, Progress and History to be non-existent, capitalism has continued to further its rational planning systems and to organise the conditions for further technological progress and anticipated accumulation, demonstrating, in other words, that Reason, Progress and History are perfectly valid concepts so long as they remain subservient to the needs of capitalist production.

SUPERSTARS

Pseudo-revolutionary literature

Working-class people are desperate to read revolutionary literature, starved of any genuine dialogue all our lives. Works of immense complexity in the fields of political economy were in enormous demand among the working classes of the nineteenth century. Bourgeois writers such as Adam Smith, David Ricardo and John Stuart Mill were bestsellers in their day and this tendency was repeated in the twentieth century with Keynes, Beveridge and recently even idiots like Will Hutton (such is the starvation of real debate being experienced by workers).

But the effect of genuine revolutionary dialogue can outweigh the immense over-production of alienated monologue spewed out daily by the mass media with just one short print-run, with one piece of graffiti, even with one cry for help.

The reason we workers currently reject so much self-styled 'revolutionary literature' is that it rejects us. It adheres to blind or patronising monologues instead of addressing us as fellow workers. It fails to request our help in the urgent task of theorising the situation of the working class (our situation) so that we can all improve our chances of sustaining and broadening any practical critique of bourgeois society which emerges in the workplaces or on the streets.

This reflects the fact that most so-called revolutionary groups are more undemocratic in structure and unaccountable in funding than the mainstream bourgeois political parties they attack.

They operate amid a secrecy they claim is necessary to protect them from the scrutiny of the security services when in reality this secrecy is intended to protect them from being scrutinised by us, the workers they patronise. The state, operating through its security agents, instantly recognises in a secretive revolutionary group a model of its own elitist structure 'in waiting'. State power can only be weakened by openness and direct democracy and as pseudo-revolutionary groups are state power in embryonic form they are in equal danger from these conditions.

They are therefore currently trying to disguise their internal hierarchies by tingeing their rhetoric with ideas they have culled from previous workers' uprisings and the councilist theorists of the 1960s and 1970s. Their hope is that these new hybrid slogans will ape the real demands and desires of the working classes closely enough to fool us.

But they are forever out-paced by the sheer originality of our contempt for the everyday life under capitalism which generates them as the last pyramid schemers we will encounter before we win our freedom.

Our great adventure

Potentially revolutionary situations lie constantly below the surface of everyday life. This is because alienation, the basis of all poverty, is a universal experience.

Today we live in a world proletarianised beyond recognition. But this means that our aims can at last become truly prodigious and vastly eclipse previous revolutionary calls for the nationalisation of factories and land, slogans nevertheless powerful enough to change armies into mutineers in their day.

Our revolutionary task as a class is now being set out for us by the bourgeoisie. It is to seize hold of their next global movement against us, the global colonisation of our leisure time and space through the subsumption of leisure under capital, and use this movement to at last make the fulfilment of our dreams and human creativity the sole democratic basis of society.

The monstrous leisure, entertainment and media industries which the bourgeoisie will increasingly try to project into power above us will merely amount to a dreadfully crippled, counterfeit version of what our own collective consciousness as a species would look like in power.

For we, as a revolutionary species, represent nature's own self-consciousness.

We enter the twenty-first century cradling in our arms the infant sciences of quantum and genetic mechanics. The current applications of these sciences are meagre abstracts serving the imperatives of capitalism. The awesome potential they offer, however, could push open the doors of perception so that we may one day be able to place the very process of evolution under our command.

We could eventually transcend the organic path of human development and replace this with a world of incredible, self-designed possibilities, become, both as individuals and as a species, so noble in reason, so infinite in faculties that we are, in our apprehension, like gods.

Capitalism, by contrast, is a system totally constrained by its need to increase our alienation, to make all of us poorer and more divorced from the purpose of our own lives for the benefit of a tiny number of billionaires. It can have no other strategy because the

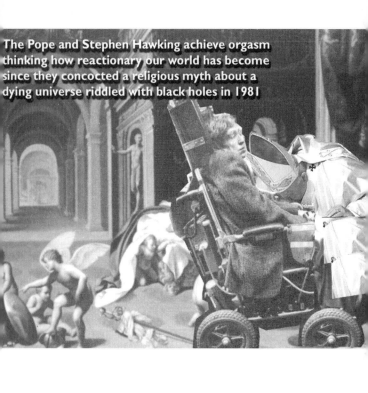

The Pope and Stephen Hawking achieve orgasm
thinking how reactionary our world has become
since they concocted a religious myth about a
dying universe riddled with black holes in 1981

intensification of alienation is the only method it has of intensifying profitable accumulation, of surviving in terms of its own alienated logic.

But this strategy provides capitalism's profound vulnerability. No matter what host of actors it assembles in front us, no matter how many television presenters, politicians, academics, pundits, journalists, advertisers, 'community representatives', middle-class 'revolutionaries' or police spokesmen it auditions to sing to us in its endless media musical of praise to everyday life under capitalism, we will always remain acutely, personally aware of our alienation, and for that reason we will always remain in a potentially revolutionary situation.

It is our task as revolutionaries to rally each other out of our personal isolation and low self-esteem and remind ourselves that this alienation is not our own individual crisis but the very economic basis of our current society.

We must never lose sight of who causes our situation until that situation can at last be made revolutionary. Before this can happen we need to become our own theorists and to defend our struggle against the ranks of bourgeois ideologists and mass-media editors who are paid to dismiss us as idiots and criminals.

But our task as workers is not just to become our own theorists but to become our own dialecticians, to overthrow bourgeois society and hierarchy in both theory and practice, to abolish private property by seizing hold of our own lives and potential and that of the technology currently owned by the bourgeoisie.

Amazingly, this great adventure is not reserved for some distant revolutionary uprising set decades into the future. It is within the grasp of all of us right now.

Eclipsing the fabricated thrill of being temporarily famous within the terms of bourgeois society, being anything from a pop star to a petty shareholder for example, is the ability for us to take part as members of a truly rank-and-file revolutionary group of our own making; an experimental and pioneering version of a democratic workers' council, a 'share-club' dedicated to the destruction of capitalist society.

At the heart of the selfish thrill of being a member of a successful rock band, board of directors or winning political party – achievements held aloft as ecstasy by our current society – lies intense loneliness, ignorance and isolation because these achievements are in reality constructed. They exclude the human race from participation except as passive spectators or victims.

Only within a truly revolutionary group can we begin to uncover our genuine personalities by living democratic, interactive lives. We can learn through electing and immediately recalling all our representatives to raise our very consciousness into power, ensuring that all positions within our society retain interchangeable, technician status and that hierarchical, bourgeois figures such as editors, directors and owners can therefore never begin to separate out above us. For if we allow any unelected privileges to develop we will surely note:

> as Anton Ciliga noted from the depths of one of Stalin's prisons, 'technical questions of organisation (in even the smallest revolutionary group) can turn out to be social questions'.[62]

Membership of a truly revolutionary group enables us to discuss and develop our critique of capitalist society and to move outwards from this towards attacking undemocratic power through the distribution of that critique.

This is the development of a truly revolutionary movement. Nothing could equal the excitement of being involved in it. I hope

---

62 *The Society of the Spectacle.*

that this manifesto will be found to contain useful enough contributions to warrant critique by such a group.

Homo sparticus

The story of the twentieth century was the story of a steadily proletarianising world, a story of peasants evacuating the countryside *en masse* and flocking into sprawling cities in every corner of our planet.

Those few who have been left behind on the land have also found themselves becoming industrialised, having to operate machinery for large agricultural companies every bit as capitalist as their urban counterparts.

And we, this assembling industrial proletariat (armed with such genius that we have been able to theorise total world revolution from our infancy as a class in the mid-nineteenth century) have always aimed at establishing worldwide classless freedom.

Because of our early numerical weaknesses we have experienced instead one hundred and fifty years of modern bourgeois revolution, often carried out against us in our own name. But, as the twenty-first century begins, we, the industrial workers of the world will soon constitute a bare majority of the human race for the first time. And so two vast classes will face each other: Them, the statistically minute but economically gigantic class of two hundred or so billionaires and the ten per cent of the world's population who make up their middle-class entourage, and Us, an immense proletariat matching the international scale of their globalised capital.

The instant any of us in this international under-class succeeds in seizing the means of production in an advanced industrial area we will outstrip our revolutionary predecessors the bourgeoisie and announce that, through our actions, we have 'destroyed the capitalist regime entirely'.

Though the rest of our class throughout the world will swiftly take up this slogan, it will hurtle into prehistoric antiquity almost as soon as it has been uttered. Because from this moment onwards we will come to embody humanity itself, starting to rise up and shed off its primitive class handicap forever. We will then emerge unified and conscious at last that we are the world-famous Revolutionary Human Race, the owners and architects of history.